Social Media Users Facing Harassment

Gregory M. Insley

ABSTRACT

Previous studies have shown that online harassment has negative psychological, physiological and economic impacts on those who experience it. This study adds to existing literature by testing the combined impacts of online harassment together in concert on users across genders. This study also adds to existing literature by examining the economic impacts that online harassment has on influencers specifically while examining this effect across genders. Social media influencers and users (N=708) were solicited to participate in a self-administered survey which measured the experience of harassment behaviors along with psychological, physiological and economic impacts. Results indicate that higher levels of harassment are associated with higher combined impacts compared to the impact of any singular type of impact alone. Gender had no impact on a respondent's likelihood of experiencing combined impacts. This study also indicates that online harassment likely has negative economic impacts for influencers whose income potential depends entirely on their engagements on social media platforms. According to terrestrial workplace harassment laws, social media corporations can be framed as liable for the harassment of the influencer population and should provide benefits to mitigate the harms experienced.

Keywords: Social media, online harassment, influencers

Table of Contents

List of Tables

Chapter One: Background and Purpose of Study

In 2019 it was estimated that over 3.4 billion people actively used social media throughout the globe (Kaur et al., 2021) with Instagram alone having more than 1 billion users (Belanche et al., 2021). Social media sites like Instagram, Discord, TikTok, Twitter, Meta (Facebook), Snapchat and YouTube are all free to access, allowing users to instantly join a vast and global user base. In these online spaces there exists the possibility for people to connect with each other, transcending the physical barriers of the terrestrial world. Social media has also become a profitable workplace, giving rise to the profession of influencing. Social media influencers can most easily be defined as opinion leaders (Belanche et al., 2021) who have an engaged following on social media. The profession becomes profitable when companies pay an influencer to promote a certain product to their audience as a marketing strategy. There is a significant amount of economic opportunity for influencers as 65% of multinational brands have invested in influencer marketing and the combined investment was estimated to be $10 billion in 2020 (Hughes et al., 2019).

As increased numbers of people continue to engage on social media globally, online harassment has become a common part of the user experience (Cross, 2019). Online harassment is used as a blanket term for online sexual harassment, cyberbullying, flaming, trolling, and cyberstalking. These behaviors are unwanted by the victim (Wilson et al., 2022: Smith, 2018) and could negatively impact the emotional, physical and economic health of those victimized. It is estimated that 30-40% of internet users will experience cyber harassment at some point (Smith, 2018). Most social media users are women (Duffy & Hund, 2019: Megara, 2014) and there is research to support that women disproportionately experience online harassment behaviors (Suzor et al., 2019: Citron, 2009: Henry & Powell, 2016: Veletsianos et al., 2018), especially those that are sexual in nature (Buchanan & Mahoney, 2022: Suzor et al., 2019). Feminist theory predicts that the gender inequalities of the terrestrial world have followed users into the online world (Are, 2020: Banet-Weiser & Miltner, 2016), accounting for the high levels of gendered harassment. Routine activity theory is a useful tool for framing how and why online spaces have become so harassment prone. United States internet legislation has allowed for platforms to be incapable guardians when it comes to protecting users from harassment. Growing research on the negative mental health impacts associated with social media use suggests that the mental health of users is deteriorating the longer they use social media, forming a group of motivated offenders. Social media is becoming an increasingly important part of people's lives and influencers are economically dependent on the social media use of others, creating a set of available victims. The current legal climate is particularly important to discuss because it allows social media corporations to be incapable guardians. Policy implications will also be explored.

There is existing research on how repeated online harassment behaviors or cyberstalking (an interchangeable term) impacts those who experience it. Maple (2011) conducted a survey-based study with the University of Bedfordshire in the United Kingdom that asked over 350 cyberstalking victims about the impacts of victimization. The results indicated that there are economic and psychological effects of cyberstalking victimization. Begotti & Maran (2019) found that there are physical (health) and emotional impacts of cyberstalking victimization. In regard to the impacts on influencers specifically, Hassan et al. (2018) conducted a small quantitative study on social media influencers that were subjected to cyberbullying and found that the consequences of victimization included negative psychological effects and the loss of career opportunity such as closing one's account and dealing with a tarnished reputation.

This study adds to the existing literature in two specific ways. First, the combined impacts of online harassment (psychological, physiological and economic) have not been tested and examined together in one study. Second, the combined effects of online harassment have not been examined across genders. More specifically, the economic impacts from online harassment on social media influencers have not been explicitly tested nor has this effect been tested across genders. Therefore, a third contribution is being added to the literature as social media influencers are economically dependent on user engagement in a way that the average user is not. Because of their difference in vulnerabilities, the experiences of social media users and social media influencers are not comparable in this study and impacts will be examined separately. Finally, research on terrestrial workplace harassment shows that there are negative emotional, physical and economic impacts associated with victimization (Salin et al., 2020). Because social media has become a workplace for influencers, it can be argued that they may be entitled to the legal protections afforded to traditional workers in the terrestrial world by the United States Civil Rights Act of 1964. The differences and similarities between the impacts of harassment on influencers and terrestrial workers will be explored in further detail.

If social media platforms are facilitating the harm of their users and those impacted are suffering economic consequences as a result, this is of a criminal nature. Social media corporations are profiting from user engagement whether it is positive or negative. Currently, online abuse that does not violate federal law is a normalized behavior that is harmful in the aggregate (Suzor et al., 2019). Criminology as a discipline is centered around exploring acts that are harmful and the context that facilitates those acts. There will likely only be increased social media use in the future (and harms as a result), not less, requiring the need for close examination of its impacts.

What constitutes crime is an ever-evolving concept. In the United States alone, slavery, lynching, spousal rape and firing someone from a job because of their gender or sexual orientation were all perfectly legal at one point. Though all these things were harmful and induced great suffering, the law permitted all these activities. Therefore, the law does not always adequately condemn what is criminal. Internet legislation is lacking in the United States when it comes to requiring social media platforms to reduce the exposure of users to the harms of online harassment. Accountability is also lacking globally as standardized, international internet legislation is lacking completely. Scholars must work to inform the law through research and create opportunities for policy improvement.

Thesis Elements

This research will explore the combined effects of online harassment on social media users. It will also examine if the combined effects of online harassment impacts are gendered. Chapter 1 was an introduction to the study and an in-depth exploration of what behaviors the term "online harassment" refers to in research. Social media use was framed as an increasingly commonplace activity and a lucrative workspace for influencing professionals. The academic contribution was introduced as there is a gap in the literature regarding how online harassment affects social media users and influencers economically, psychologically and physiologically. Online harassment has been known to have negative impacts on other professions that leverage social media and considering that influencers spend a lot of time online, economic impacts on this population should be understood. Because social media has become a workplace for influencers, online harassment as a type of workplace harassment was introduced.

Chapter 2 will consist of an in-depth literature review that examines the prevalence and impacts of social media use. Next, there will be an examination of the research highlighting the prevalence and impacts of online harassment with sections detailing the online harassment of influencers and findings that suggest that online harassment impacts female users more often. An exploration of workplace harassment and sexual harassment will take place, followed by analysis as to what the impacts are. Workplace harassment research and definitions will be compared to the experience of an influencer working online and dealing with harassment behaviors. A review of terrestrial workplace harassment law will be compared to internet legislation (both domestically and internationally) in order to explore why it is difficult to address and reduce online harassment. Feminist theory and routine activity theory will be explored as an explanation as to why online harassment, especially gendered online harassment is so prevalent. At the end of the chapter, research questions and hypotheses to be tested in the study will be introduced.

In chapter 3, all data collection methodologies will be explored along with a detailed description of variables and the sources of various scales being used. Chapter 4 will include sample descriptives and the presentation of OLS regression models used to test hypotheses. Chapter 5 will discuss the fundings of the study, providing detailed explanations for results based on theory and other facts presented in the literature review. Policy implications from this study will be proposed, followed by a discussion of the study limitations and their potential impact of the study's results. Suggestions for future research will be provided. Finally, a summary of findings and how they address the academic contribution will conclude the thesis.

Chapter Two: Literature Review

Influencers

Social media has brough fourth an entirely new type of profession. Influencers are self-employed entities that create content on social media that generates revenue. Influencing as a career has a multitude of benefits. For example, viable platforms like Instagram, YouTube and TikTok are all free to access. Outside of having an internet connection and a device that is capable of recording video or taking photos, no other equipment is needed to begin a career as an influencer. The barrier to entry is relatively low-cost and low risk. Employment as an influencer has a low-barrier access level because it does not require any advanced skills or educational qualifications. There is instant potential to engage a large global audience, and the ability to be self-employed can be empowering for individuals. With influencing, there is no daily commute, reporting to a boss, filling out a timecard or working directly with co-workers. It is a career choice that allows for a high level of independence from traditional employment structures. Though there are a considerable number of people who make a living just off their influencing capabilities, there is very little data available on what the average influencer generates in revenue (Trotter, 2020).

An influencer can profit from their social media account in a variety of ways. These can include corporate sponsorships to promote a product, affiliate links (essentially a pay per click ad where the influencer gets commissions) and user subscriptions to exclusive content (Bradley, 2022). The influencer payment structure is not straightforward and varies per platform and individual marketing contract. Each marketing contract (or sponsorship) that a company offers to an influencer must consider their number of followers and engagement metrics as platforms have formulas on the minimum salary that influencers can be paid based on these criteria (Bradley,

2022). The highly variable payment structure and payment avenues make calculating income for the average influencer very difficult, if not impossible. Meta (Facebook), who owns Instagram invested $1 Billion dollars into influencers in the year 2022 by creating various incentive programs, monetary bonus structures for views on videos called "reels," and, other money-making ventures that are still being developed (Bradley, 2022). Social media corporations want influencers to make money so in turn, they also continue to make money by keeping users engaged on their platform. Influencing is a promising career option that has few barriers to entry and the potential for financial success. While this may seem like an easy career choice, there are downsides to frequent social media use and the growing prevalence of online harassment can certainly be labeled as a negative aspect of the profession. Influencers may be participating in the deterioration of their own mental health and also of those who follow them.

Adverse Outcomes of Social Media Use

There is a strong body of research which reveals that social media use has negative outcomes for those who use it both generally and excessively. Woods & Scott (2016) surveyed 800 adolescents in Scotland and found that those who reported being more emotionally invested in social media experienced higher levels of anxiety, depression and poor sleep quality. Bhargava & Velasquez (2021) note that internet addiction in general is correlated to a decrease in academic performance, causing younger populations to feel stressed and a lack of self-esteem. A longitudinal study by Steinsbekk & Wichstrøm et al., (2021) found that among girls' self-esteem decreases over time based on their social media use. Lastly, Craig et al., (2020) examined the social media behaviors of 180,919 adolescents in 42 countries and concluded that cyber-bullying perpetration was more commonly reported than victimization for both boys and girls, indicating that children are meaner to each other online than offline. Considering that social media use is becoming a common part of everyday life, it is likely that these patterns of low self-esteem, anxiety, depression and bullying behaviors will continue being observed, but in subsequently younger populations with each passing year.

While the harms are well-established, other research suggests the possible positive impacts of social media interactions. A study done by Valkenburg, Koutamanis & Vossen (2017) found that positive comments from friends on social media did appear to increase the self-esteem of the adolescent respondents. Therefore, if interactions on social media are positive, theoretically social media use could be a benefit to a younger user. However, given the prevalence of online harassment, this is likely not a common reality for most users. The perceived prevalence of online harassment will be discussed in a later section.

Though much of the academic research on social media harms focuses on children and adolescents, it is important to note that an estimated 80% of adults in the United States use social media (Pozzar et al., 2020) and that social media addiction has been labeled as a global problem among young adults (Bhargava & Velasquez, 2021). Mitropoulou, Karagianni & Thomadakis (2022) surveyed 255 Greek adults and found that people who exhibit more self-compassion are less likely to exhibit social media addiction as they spend less time on social media websites and report being healthier overall. Those who were labeled as self-compassionate individuals also reported self-kindness, self-acceptance, and mindfulness which help to regulate negative feelings and behaviors. Social media addiction is an increasingly common problem that is associated with negative mental health outcomes and unregulated emotions, then those who spend increased time online may be more likely to behave negatively towards others (Craig et al., 2022: Mitropoulou, Karagianni & Thomadakis, 2022). Therefore, on the current trajectory, online harassment behaviors will likely increase as internet access also continues to increase throughout the world.

The reason that social media addiction will likely increase overtime has to do with platform design. The business model of social media can be simplified to state that the longer a user spends time online, the more advertising revenue platforms make (Walter, 2022). Therefore, what becomes important for revenue is showing users content that they will engage with for long periods of time. The invention of the "like" button is an example of how some platforms are collecting data on the preferences of users; if a user likes a certain content type, platform algorithms respond by continuing to show other content that is related to that original like (Bhargava & Velasquez, 2021: Walter, 2022). On a global level, users are more often engaged by content that is inflammatory thereby causing an increased circulation and reward for creating content that is negative and makes people angry (Walter, 2022). Not only is increased internet use harmful for user wellbeing, but social media content that is most popular also happens to be the most negative and extreme (Walter, 2022).

Inflammatory content circulation combined with declining mental health has created an adverse environment on social media. Corporations have no financial incentive (Walter, 2022) nor legal incentive to reduce the harm that their platforms create and perpetuate. Adaptive algorithms are efficient at constantly showing users the content that most interests them (Bhargava & Velasquez, 2021) therefore, keeping them online longer. Research has shown that keeping users on the platform longer is likely to worsen their mental health (Raudsepp & Kais, 2019: Shakya & Christakis, 2017) Therefore, influencers may be engaging follower populations that exhibit low self-compassion, low self-esteem, unregulated emotions and a propensity towards exhibiting bullying behaviors. Social media may continue to addict and harm more people with each passing year, causing online audiences to become sadder, meaner and more abusive towards others.

Online Harassment Section

Prevalence of Online Harassment

Many studies have examined the prevalence and impacts of online harassment, yet the behaviors included for study are not standardized in research (Wilson et al., 2022). Behaviors of online harassment are many and can include blanket terms such as cyberstalking, cyberbullying, or specific acts such as doxing or catfishing. Simply put, online harassment is any behavior that is purposefully abusive, unwanted by the victim and occurs more than once (Cross, 2019). It is with this broad definition that online harassment will be explored throughout this paper and, recently, it was estimated that 64% of United States adults under 30 years and under have experienced online harassment (Pew Research Center, 2021) at some point. Research suggests that experiencing online harassment behaviors (bullying, sexual harassment, cyberstalking) is especially common for adolescents (Copp et al., 2021) and that the impacts of harassment victimization are similar to the impacts of excessive use such as depressive symptoms and low self-esteem. Copp et al., (2021) surveyed 1,152 adolescents (ages 10-18) who use social media in the United States and found that 37% of the sample reported being cyberbullied and 15% reported experiencing sexual harassment.

Begotti & Maran (2019) surveyed 250 students at the University of Torino and found that most of their sample had experienced multiple types of cyberstalking behaviors and that depressive symptoms were statistically significant. Anxiety symptoms were found to be insignificant. The impacts of cyberstalking were operationalized utilizing two scales titled "physical symptoms" and "emotional symptoms." This research showcased that victims of cyberstalking can experience impacts that are physical and psychological. These phenomena manifest differently from each other but, both are harmful. Physical health and mental health are equally important, and it is essential to understand that cyberstalking has measurable negative health impacts. In this study, the impacts across genders were not examined or reported (Begotti & Maran, 2019).

Gendered Online Harassment

There is a body of literature supporting that online abuse is more often aimed at women and that women and girls are experiencing most of the sexual violence victimization online (Henry & Powell, 2016: Suzor et al., 2019). Social media exacerbates harassment behaviors in general (Adams, 2018) and this is likely as a result of the negative mental health impacts on users explored in earlier sections (Mitropoulou, Karagianni & Thomadakis, 2022: Craig et al., 2020: Raudsepp & Kais, 2019). The disproportionate amount of harassment that females experience on the internet could be attributed to the gender inequality of the terrestrial world (Henry & Powell, 2016: Suzor et al., 2019). Angus Reid (2016) found in their study that Canadian women, when compared to men, are twice as likely to endure extreme abuse online such as cyberstalking and sexual harassment. Within the field of journalism specifically, online victimization likelihood increases for women who publicly display their true identities to promote their work (Veletsianos et al., 2018).

Online attacks aimed at female journalists has been a well-studied topic in legal and sociological research. Adams (2018) found that many inflammatory and abusive comments aimed at female journalists were in response to those writing about feminist topics or directed at those covering traditionally male topics such as video games or sports. However, the covering of feminist topics by female journalists is also unwelcome and sparks inflammatory comments and messages (Adams, 2018). Such studies focus on female journalists who are also required to have an online presence, making their work logistically similar to that of an influencer. The key difference is that journalists are employed by organizations that should protect them from the harassment that they receive online. Research has shown that female journalists are harassed online far more often than male journalists and receive little support for corrective action from social media platforms or from their employers (Eberspacher, 2019).

Unfortunately, as many as one in five technology journalists decline to put their identities on certain pieces as a protective measure against harassment (Adams, 2018). Studies also found that some female journalists will turn down covering certain stories, especially in male-dominated spaces such as sports (Eberspacher, 2019), to protect themselves from anticipated online abuse and vitriol thus limiting their career progression (Adams, 2018: Eberspacher, 2019: Carlson & Witt, 2020). Female influencers may also avoid certain topics or turn down certain advertisement deals utilizing similar self-preservation logic. If found to be true, the careers of yet another group of female professionals are being impeded online because of gendered harassment. Because online engagement has become essential to a journalist's success, female journalists are disadvantaged and must overcome gendered barriers (Eberspacher, 2019). Unlike female influencers, female journalists sometimes have the option not to disclose their identities. But, this could be detrimental to the success of a career where exposure matters.

Another group of female professionals whose online harassment has received some attention in research is that of female academics. Vera-Gray (2017), studied the online harassment of feminist female researchers within different Facebook groups and concluded that men see (feminist) female scholars as an unworthy intrusion into the historically male space of academia. They also wanted to understand how men intruded on feminist spaces online. These digital spaces online are often attacked with misogynistic-focused abuse. Veletsianos et al. (2018) found that most female scholars who are attacked online were not well protected by their institutions in response to online abuse. Essentially, the institutions that they worked for took no action to protect these women to reduce the amount of vitriol they were facing online. Those victimized reported feelings of self-blame and minimized their exposure as a self-protective measure. ***Influencer Harassment***

Because social media influencers must engage online to generate income, it is unlikely that they will be able to avoid online harassment given its prevalence. There are very few studies that examine the harassment of social media influencers specifically, but they do provide some insight as to how this population is harassed. Hassan et al. (2018) conducted a small qualitative study of 20 influencers and published preliminary findings of just 7 interviews. They identified harassment themes that aligned with the scale generated by Wilson et al (2022) such as repeated unwanted messages (flaming), Catfishing (pretending to be someone they were not) and exposing private information to others without consent (outing). The impacts and consequences of experiencing these behaviors reported by Hassan et al., included lost opportunities (account closure, lost corporate sponsorships), loss of followers (revenue potential) and psychological effects such as stress, anxiety, depression, loss of self-esteem and sleep (Hassan et al., 2018). Though this study is small and based on preliminary findings only, there appears to be economic and psychological impacts associated with the harassment of social media influencers.

As observed by Hassan et al., (2018), harassment may have measurable mental and financial impacts on influencers. Because influencers have to work on social media with a user audience, they are economically vulnerable to the impacts of harassment (Hassan et al., 2018). This irremovable vulnerability sets them apart from other users on social media. Therefore, online harassment could be considered a form of workplace harassment. If online harassment yields economic consequences for influencers, it may mirror the negative impacts of workplace harassment in the terrestrial world. If this is the case, influencing carries some of the same potential harassment downsides that come with working in person at a company, without any of the nationally mandated legal protections and internal policies that a traditionally employed people may have to lean on. Exploration on the impacts of terrestrial workplace harassment will be discussed and explored next, in order to examine if the impacts and consequences could potentially apply to influencers in the online workspace.

Terrestrial Workplace Harassment

Because influencing is a profession, is it possible that harassment online impacts this population in a similar way that it would impact an employee in the terrestrial world? To explore this question, the prevalence and impact of terrestrial workplace harassment must be understood. Like online harassment, workplace harassment also has a variety of overlapping terms such as workplace bullying, workplace sexual harassment, workplace discrimination and incivility (Patel, 2021). Workplace sexual harassment and workplace bullying will be the terms explored in this section to understand the prevalence and impacts of terrestrial workplace harassment to examine if the scenarios and consequences present any alignment with the potential experiences of influencers.

Workplace bullying can be defined as the repeated systematic mistreatment of an employee or employees in the workplace (Salin et al., 2020). It is estimated that a minimum of 15% of employees experience harassment at the global level (Boudrias, Trépanier & Salin, 2021: Nielsen & Einarsen, 2018) However, despite 30 years of research on workplace bullying, very little is known about its true prevalence worldwide (Hodgins et al., 2020). Nielsen & Einarsen (2018) examined 91 studies on the impacts of workplace bullying. The literature examined strongly supports that workplace bullying is associated with post-traumatic stress symptoms,

depression, anxiety, increased risk for physical disease, and low job satisfaction. Nielsen &
Einarsen (2018) label these impacts as "robust" for they have been replicated across many
different studies that examined different occupations, countries and cultures. Patel (2021) also
reported economic impacts from workplace bullying such as monetary loss from lack of
promotion, loss of wages from taking time off to recover and, loss of wages from quitting
without having another source of income readily available. Therefore, harassment at work
negatively impacts people in personal and professional ways. And though these impacts are well
documented in research, protecting employees from workplace bullying through legislation has
not been effective (Hodgins et al., 2020). Speculation as to why will be explored in the criminal-
legal section.

Workplace harassment of a sexual nature also appears to be gendered as to mirror the
harassment levels of the online world. Terrestrial workplace sexual harassment prevalence is
difficult to measure accurately because of under-reporting and the lack of a standardized
definition in research (Johnson et al., 2018). Current published work suggests that workplace
harassment of a sexual nature disproportionately impacts women (Folke et al., 2020) and that
women who hold workplace authority (managerial leadership and higher) or women who work
in male dominated fields experience higher levels of workplace sexual harassment (Folke et al.,
2020: Raj, Johns & Jose, 2020).

More than 2 in 5 employed women, compared to 1 in 8 employed men, have experienced
sexual harassment at their place of work (Raj, Johns & Jose, 2020). These numbers are likely
smaller than the real figures because it is estimated that very few people report their experiences
formally to human resources or an external body (Johnson et al., 2018). Sexual workplace
harassment includes behaviors such as verbal slurs, sexual descriptions of a person's body, *quid*

pro quo acts, repeated calls or texts, sending an unsolicited sexual picture, physical touching without consent, and sexual assault (Raj, Johns & Jose, 2020). Women who experience sexual harassment at work, across a variety of disciplines, report lower job satisfaction, silent quitting, stress, depression, anxiety and low self-esteem (Johnson et al., 2018). Though all these impacts are very harmful and likely place barriers to women achieving workplace promotions, less than 13% of the 610 women in Raj, Johns & Jose's (2020) study reported leaving their jobs to avoid the sexually harassing behaviors. This implies that the harassment is not excluding most women from the workplace but may place barriers in front of their career trajectory potential as workplace harassment has been known to decrease a woman's chances of climbing the corporate ladder (Boudrias et al, 2021). Workplace harassment is linked to psychological, physiological and economic impacts for those victimized. Though unfortunate, there is an attempt with legislation in the United States to ensure that terrestrial workers do not experience harassment or have options for retribution when they do. Influencers do not have any such legislation to lean on. A detailed explanation of workplace and internet legislation will be discussed in the next chapter.

Legal Section

Terrestrial Workplace Harassment Laws

The United States passed the Civil Rights Act of 1964, the Age Discrimination in Employment Act of 1967, (ADEA), and the Americans with Disabilities Act of 1990, (ADA) yet none of these federal laws explicitly label workplace bullying as illegal (de las Casas, 2019). Instead, the legislations establish protected classes such as sex, age, religion and disability status which make the harassment of a person based on these specific qualities illegal at their place of work. A corporation may be held liable for the harassment of an employee when the harassment (based on a specified protected class) negatively interferes with their work in a way that results in the loss of the employee's wages, promotion, termination, their resignation, or when the employer fails to correct and discontinue the harassing behavior (Equal Employment Opportunity Commission). If an employee is being harassed or bullied for characteristics not based on a protected class, there is likely no effective legal recourse at their disposal. Therefore, federal policy to prevent and reduce workplace bullying can be very ineffective if a harmed employee fails to define their experiences within the confines of a protected class. This is very limiting as it can be hard to prove where harassment stems from if the harasser is not stating outright offenses based on a protected class.

In academic environments, female employees are protected by Title IX which states that women must have equal access to education. Sex discrimination in enrollment, participation in sports, and the distribution of student loans is not legal in the United States. Title IX also demands an academic environment that is free from sexual harassment. Females who are career academics are entitled to the same protections and provisions of Title IX as their students. However, it is important to note that Title IX defines sexual harassment as conduct that is unwanted, sexual in nature and denies a student the ability to fully participate in any aspect of an educational program (Johnson et al, 2018). Therefore, gendered harassment like crude remarks or non-sexual gender-based insults are not specifically barred under Title IX. However, females employed in academia are still entitled to the protections of Title VII because universities receive federal funds.

Internal, organization-specific policy is currently how most companies attempt to deal with workplace harassment (Hodgins et al., 2020). Salin et al., (2020) surveyed 214 human resource professionals from 14 different countries and found that most organizations view workplace bullying as a financial liability that has long-term monetary costs due to loss of productivity, turnover, negative employee attitudes and potential litigation risk. Workplace bullying is widely viewed in terms of neoliberal impacts and not necessarily in terms of the social harms that a multitude of studies have indicated that it causes (Nielsen & Einarsen, 2018: Salin et al., 2020). In addition to federal protections, individual corporations attempt to provide internal protections against workplace mistreatment (Hodgins et al., 2020: Salin et al., 2020).

Internal anti-bullying policies within corporations can be framed to mirror the "community guidelines" on social media platforms (Galpin, 2022), as they both work to discourage negative treatment of others that is separate from formal legislation. Though legal and informal policies appear to be ineffective at reducing harassment in the terrestrial world (Hodgins et al., 2020) and online, can federal workplace protection laws for terrestrial workers in the United States be interpreted in a way that could also extend these protections to influencers? Instagram, Meta and YouTube are American corporations that profit from the work of influencers. Though influencers are not technically employees of these organizations, they generate their income from and work through these organizations. The corporations also benefit financially from their participation, placing a financial incentive on the platform to help influencers perform well at work.

Arguably then, influencers should receive the same workplace harassment protections as employees in the terrestrial world. However, liability is difficult to determine as the harassment of an influencer is not coming from a co-worker or a supervisor. Influencers are technically self-employed and are subjected to harassment by fellow users of the site. And even though influencers may experience the same consequences from bullying behaviors as that of terrestrial employees like financial loss and resignation, there are no federal protections for them to gain retribution. The United States currently has no federal workplace legislation to protect influencers from harassment, even when the harassment violated that of a protected class. As previously mentioned, online harassment likely disproportionately impacts women worldwide (Suzor et al., 2019). It is likely then, that female influencers experience higher levels of harassment when compared to male influencers. Yet, a female influencer simply must deal with sexism and mistreatment if she wants to continue being an influencer. The legal situation of social media corporations allows harassment to flourish with little to no legal or financial incentive to make it stop. Therefore, influencers are subjected to a lack of workplace protections and legally mandated platform protections. The reason there is no obligation for platforms to protect general users or influencers from user harassment will be explored next.

Criminal-Legal Barriers to Reducing Harassment

There are several factors that make it difficult to criminalize and reduce online harassment worldwide. When considering the legal arguments from the previous section, even though influencers technically work on American social media platforms, except for TikTok as it is a Chinese platform, they are not provided with the protections granted by Title VII of the Civil Rights Act of 1964 which makes discrimination and harassment based on gender illegal at someone's place of employment. Committing acts of gender discrimination is not federally illegal outside of the physical workplace, therefore gender discrimination is not federally illegal online. Social media platforms are not legally obligated (by the government) to remove sexist content or punish the user who posted it. Consequently, the legal framework of the internet has fostered an unfiltered climate protected by an individual's rights to free speech online (Smith, 2018).

Barriers to Reducing Harassment on Social Media

Gendered cyber harassment creates a hostile work environment for those whose careers exist purely in the online world. Harassment at work, especially sexual harassment, is illegal in terrestrial workplaces under United States Federal Law. Also, anti-cyberstalking laws currently exist in all fifty states (Smith, 2018). However, this does not mean that they are effective in preventing or reducing cyberstalking victimization. American corporations are legally obligated to protect their employees from harassment though not all have distinct policies in place for when the harassment is committed through social media between employees who work at the same corporation (Scarduzio et al., 2021). Considering that the internet has become a workplace where writers, influencers, and authors of other mediums generate their income, the inability to speak freely without harassment repercussions is a major violation of agency. Influencers are technically self-employed entities that do not work under a corporation that is legally obligated to step in and put a stop to any harassment that they experience.

Law enforcement has proven incapable or unwilling to investigate and adjudicate online harassment cases until it is too late and the harassment transitions offline (Citron, 2009). The anonymity of online perpetrators and the advanced skills required to obtain their identities has proven to be a major obstacle for law enforcement agencies Henry et al., (2020). On the internet platform side, constant reporting and flagging of online abuse content creates a daunting amount of work as the volume of content on social media is unimaginably vast (Farid, 2018). The current workforce in charge of responding to user complaints likely cannot keep up with the amount of flagged content. Artificial intelligence and machine learning technologies are slowly being developed but they are a long way off from being efficient enough to handle the content monitoring on their own (Farid, 2018). Until then, social media platforms cannot and likely will not, until the law changes, respond to online abuse reports and complaints in a way that ends the behavior (Eberspacher, 2019) if they even respond at all (al-Khateeb et al., 2017).

Keeping oneself safe online has unintentionally become the user's responsibility and all tracking and reporting responsibilities primarily fall on the individual. Henry, et al. (2020) state that inconsistent laws, a lack of police resources, evidentiary limitations, rapid technology evolution, jurisdictional boundaries, and victim-blaming or harm minimization attitudes as the main barriers that make it difficult for law enforcement to act against perpetrators of online harassment. Because perpetrators of online harassment are making threats behind a screen, police often see this as a lack of evidence and as the actions of a non-tangible perpetrator who is unlikely capable of causing physical harm to the victim (al-Khateeb et al., 2017).

Internet platforms also present a challenge when it comes to reducing online harassment. Because social media platforms provide the space where online harassment is occurring, they appear to hold the most advantageous position to both identify and remove harassment perpetrators. However, al-Khateeb et al. (2017) found that platforms are not efficient at removing harmful content. In their study conducted with over 250 cyberstalking victims, respondents reported that internet service providers often refused to remove abusive content from their sites or simply ignored the removal requests entirely. Social media companies do have user policies that address hate speech and harassment (Galpin, 2022), often referred to as "community guidelines," that are meant to discourage users from participating in harassment and cyberstalking. However, they function as guidelines and are not effective in reducing harassment and cyberstalking victimization. Community guidelines are not effectively enforced due to the endless generation of content, which is too large to be manually monitored and the leniency provided by Section 230 of the Communications Decency Act (CDA).

Internet Policy Section

United States Policy: Section 230 of the CDA.

Section 230 of the Communications Decency Act states that no internet service provider can be held liable for what a user posts, even if the content is not constitutionally protected. (Leary, 2018). In other words, Section 230 established an important distinction between publisher and platform by protecting Internet Service Providers from being held responsible even when they fail to remove harmful content posted by third parties (Bolson, 2016; Leary, 2018). Social media platforms are categorized as internet service providers within the context of Section 230. Developers of content or independent users are considered out of the platform's control and platforms are not liable for the user content published on their sites. All that is required of internet service providers is that they act in "good faith" to remove harmful content when they come across it (Communications Decency Act, 1996). The "good faith" clause is not operationalized in any specific, measurable, or actionable way. Such vague language ultimately makes it difficult to take legal action against internet corporations when they take no action against user harassment reports. For example, Section 230 provides broad immunity for the publishing of third-party content on websites if it is assumed that they are not intentionally allowing the harm to occur. Yet, it is challenging to place legal liability on websites that facilitate online harassment because the measure of what "evidence" can be used to prove that they act in "good faith" is unclear. Companies can claim that they are policing content on their websites in support of good faith, yet what constitutes "policing" is not explicitly defined (Spiccia, 2013).

Section 230 emerged as part of a larger effort to regulate the internet. In 1996, the CDA was enacted as an attempt to shield children from encountering obscene materials on the limited (but expanding) world wide web. As Internet use became more prominent in everyday life,

Congress showed concerns about the unyielding ability of the internet to spread or expose children to obscene material, resulting in the first effort to regulate pornographic materials shown on Internet sites (Murica, 2020). The CDA's intended regulation of pornographic material on the internet sparked vocal concerns regarding the protection of free speech under the First Amendment, most notably in the 1997 Supreme Court case Reno v. the ACLU (Murica, 2020). In Reno v. the ACLU, concerns regarding free speech emerged as a response to the anti-indecency elements proposed in the CDA. The ACLU argued that the CDA violated the First Amendment by censoring expression and advocated that the terms "indecent" or "patently offensive" were too vague to be effectively applied (Sevanian, 2014). Ultimately, the Supreme court agreed and removed language that prohibited the sharing of indecent materials (Leary, 2018). As a result of the supreme court decision, the United States federal government is legally unable to tell social media companies which pieces of content to delete unless it directly violates a specific federal law.

While the CDA was seen by lawmakers as violating free speech, the addition of Section 230 helped the CDA pass as it protected the free speech of users and the liabilities of companies that provided platforms for posting (Cramer, 2020). An unintended consequence of the congressional decision to shield internet companies so broadly under Section 230 is that it protects both positive and negative posts equally (Spiccia, 2013). Stated differently, Section 230 aims to protect well-intentioned companies that fail to remove illicit content due to being unaware of its existence on their sites. On the other hand, the CDA simultaneously protects the companies that are now able to ignore or refuse to remove illicit content. Section 230 has made it legally acceptable for widespread harm on the internet to exist undetected and potentially unremovable even when reported so long as it does not directly violate federal law. By adding

Section 230, the Communications Decency Act has allowed online harassment, cyberstalking, and technology-facilitated gendered violence to thrive in tandem with the increasing scale of the online world.

In the era of internet infancy, lawmakers had a strong desire not to impede the growth of the internet and preserve a competitive free market where the internet could flourish, free of government scrutiny. Considering that the internet was a small-scale operation in 1996, the "good faith" clause was implemented with the reasoning that startups needed to avoid being shut down long enough to thrive while still being able to shield the innocent from obscene materials (Murica, 2020). The amount of content online was also theoretically more manageable at the time as the volume was lower. Section 230 helped alleviate platforms' fears about having to engage in content moderation as well as minimizing the cost of facilitating content distribution (Skorup, & Huddleston, 2020). Arguably, this liability exemption has allowed the internet to scale into what it has become in the modern day.

Threats, lewd comments, and discrimination do not receive first amendment protections. But, Section 230 has made it possible for internet service providers to avoid the gargantuan task of meticulously scrubbing their platforms for all of these abuses that are posted. The good faith loophole does not provide specific requirements for the removal of illegal content, internet service providers only need to try. When the law punishes an online harassment perpetrator for targeting individuals based on their protected class, for example, gender, no First Amendment protections would be violated (Citron, 2009). The federal government could theoretically order a social media platform to remove abuses of this kind. Internet service providers could operate under this assumption and make their platforms more hospitable by removing posts that contain threats or libel. Yet, most platforms do not and likely choose not to invest in the resources that would allow them to do so in a timely manner. Therefore, the United States has created a situation where online harassment can flourish and social media platforms do not have to take specific, measure steps towards reducing it.

International Internet Policy

The internet legal situation in the United States is important to mention because this country holds the highest concentration of internet corporations (Suzor et al., 2019). Instagram, Facebook, YouTube and Twitter are all American corporations. However as previously mentioned, social media use is a global phenomenon and legal requirements for online behavior vary per each nation state. This presents a complex situation as jurisdictional boundaries and nation sovereignty make internet legislation difficult to create and enforce consistently worldwide. Therefore, universal online behavior laws are not only nonexistent but impossible to universally implement if they did. And though there is no exact policy, the United Nations still has desired expectations for corporations that do business on a global scale. They created the Guiding Principles on Business and Human rights in 2011, which is a series of recommendations and guidelines for how businesses ought to operate in order to ensure the uplifting of human rights in each country in which they operate (Suzor et al., 2019). Essentially, no business operating internationally is supposed to cause harm where they infiltrate. This documentation was written as a referable guideline and is by no means enforceable legislation. No corporation of any kind is obligated to follow the guidelines. Though the document was written in 2011, in the very early stages of social media development, principles can still be applied to internet corporations. As referenced in previous literature, the mental health impacts of social media use and online harassment negatively impact users outside of the United States.

Rapp (2021) argues that when social media is used as a tool for human rights abuses like genocide, it is the responsibility of the "home state" to intervene. For example, they articulate that it was the obligation of the United States to force Facebook (Meta) to stop operating in Myanmar (formerly known as Burma) when the platform became a tool used by political elites to incite genocide against the Rohingya people. Though this may seem like a logical expectation, Facebook was notified multiple times of their platform's involvement in both genocidal incitement and the coordination of violent acts (Walter, 2022) but chose to do nothing about it. International legislation does not legally require platforms to prevent or stop violations of human rights when operating abroad (Rapp, 2021). Though the use of social media to commit acts of genocide is extreme, this example highlights just how little legal responsibility social media corporations have worldwide, even when the connections to crime are clear and the consequences are dire.

The International Covenant on Civil and Political Rights (ICCPR) is concerned with an individual's right to use the internet freely (Land, 2013). Article 13 specifically is concerned with ensuring that states do not interfere with an individual's right to access uncensored information online and participate in the use of the technology (Land, 2013). With the right to use internet telecommunications established as an international human right, stopping individual users leveraging internet platforms to harm others becomes very difficult. The global emphasis on protecting free speech, a lack of international internet legislation, and a lack of accountability within United States legislation makes it nearly impossible to hold social media corporations accountable when their platforms cause harm, in the United States or elsewhere.

Research has already revealed that online harassment causes harm on a global level (Begotti et al., 2019: Maple et al., 2011). Several studies in a multitude of countries have revealed that victimization can impact a person mentally and physically. There is no legislation (global or domestic) that forces social media companies to reduce incidents of online harassment. The lack of required content monitoring by social media platforms in the United States, sanctioned by Section 230 of the CDA, has created an environment where harassment harms those who use social media. A lack of policy to address this reality means that social media corporations are profiting from the harm of their users. Now that the legal reasons as to why social media has been allowed to become a place of harassment and vitriol on a global scale, academic theory will be applied to analyze and predict the negative behaviors of individual users being observed from the harassment studies in the literature review.

Theory

Applying Feminist Theory

Feminist theory aims to examine and critique the female experience within a predominantly patriarchal society. There is an intense focus on the injustices that women face within a broader structural system which favors patriarchy and often, various strategies for social change are presented (Daly & Chesney-Lind, 1988). Gender is seen as not a phenomenon but a social construction that orders social interactions in a very tangible way (Daly & Chesney-Lind, 1988). Intersectional feminist theory clusters a person's overlapping identities such as race, class position, gender identity and sexual orientation when examining their specific experiences and challenges. These attributes for each person can follow them from the terrestrial world, into their online profile. Especially if that person decides to showcase their true selves on social media. As internet access continues to spread, the diversity of social media users will only increase. The intersections of their identities will likely impact them online as they would in the terrestrial world because the terrestrial world and the online world are not truly separate spaces but places where users can live in both simultaneously (Lazarus, 2019). Therefore, the concepts of feminist theory developed in the terrestrial world can be applied to the structures and situations of the online word as well.

Criminology has largely disregarded gender in its analysis of digital crimes (Lazarus, 2019). Bellini et al. (2022) argue that a feminist lens can add value to the developing field of Human Computer Interaction (HCI). HCI seeks to understand what it means to digitize the human experience (Bellini et al., 2022) and gender constructs are a facet of human experience. Feminist theory is needed in the design and deployment of emerging technologies (Bellini et al., 2022) because technology is not morally neutral and can express the biases and internalized social constructions of its creators (Suzor et al., 2019). Until the online experience is developed with gender inequality in mind, gender inequality will follow female users from the offline world into the online world. The disproportionate harassment levels of women online are likely the result of broader, offline societal practices and values (Lazarus, 2019) manifesting themselves online. Because of this reality, when it comes to examining gender relations within cybercrime, Lazarus (2019) recommends using the Tripartite Cyber-crime Framework (TCF) as this methodology examines the motivations behind certain types of victimization. The three umbrellas of victimization include socioeconomic, psychosocial, and geopolitical.

Online harassment falls under the "psychosocial" as it aims to harm victims psychologically. Psychological harm has been known to have economic impact on those victimized (Lazarus, 2019). Socioeconomic in this study refers to identity theft or the exploitation of personal information but arguably, online harassment may cause users to invest money in certain coping mechanisms from online harassment as observed in the Maple et al., (2011) and Begotti et al. (2019). Feminist theory would predict that the psychological and economic impact from online harassment will impact women more severely because gender inequality in the terrestrial world is contributing to the disproportionate harassment levels in the online world. Understanding this relationship could provide evidence of unequal opportunity and gender discrimination in the social media workplace.

As previously mentioned, most social media users are women (Duffy & Hund, 2019: Megarry, 2014) and it is also true that most social media influencers are female (Duffy & Hund, 2019). Not surprisingly, women are disproportionately experiencing severe harassment victimization online (Pew Research Center, 2021: Suzor et al., 2019) where they are the dominant group. Social media can be place where women are empowered to speak out against the gender inequality of the terrestrial world (Malik & Sinha, 2022) like in the case of the #metoo movement that began on Twitter. Despite the disproportionate harassment levels, social media can still be a valuable communication tool for women. A woman who lives in an oppressive patriarchal culture could theoretically voice their opinions online in a way that they could likely never do offline. The troublesome social problem is that though women are succeeding and participating on social media, it may come at a cost to their mental and economic wellbeing. Some social media platforms could be an exception to gender barriers, as profiles can be anonymized, yet it has developed into an additional space where women are commonly subjected to the negative impacts of gender inequality. Eckert (2018) suggests that gendered online abuse is most accurately examined through a feminist lens as the online world inherited the social constructs of gender from the terrestrial world. The high levels of online harassment experienced by women can likely be framed as the direct transcendence of gendered inequalities traveling from the offline world into the online world (Lazarus, 2019). Gender based discrimination, even online, has the potential to form similar barriers to economic and social success observed in the terrestrial world (Suzor et al., 2019).

Zimmerman (2017) argues that feminist theorists should cease to separate the offline and online worlds when analyzing the impacts of gender inequality. Gendered harassment online runs the risk of economic exclusion in modern times as an online presence is often beneficial for a person's professional success. Being able to participate on social media is becoming essential to the pursuit of economic, academic, and social opportunities (Eckert, 2018: Veletsianos et al., 2018). The reason influencers are important to examine within this framework is that their livelihoods depend entirely on being available for public internet interactions (Duffy & Hund, 2019). They simply cannot make their accounts private because this limits their ability to gain followers and caps their income potential. Influencers, especially female influencers, may face more economic impacts from online harassment when compared to male influencers. Unlike terrestrial professions, they cannot simply switch companies (and do the same job) to improve their working conditions.

Perceived gender roles may influence the levels of harassment that female influencers face. This may influence the online harassment perpetrated by both men and women. Duffy et al. (2022) examined hateful comments directed at influencers by both men and women and discovered that there are themes to common audience frustrations. These include that influencers are untalented and undeserving of their success, they are inauthentic when adverting products, and that many female influencers are promoting unrealistic lifestyle expectations for women (Duffy et al., 20202). There may be a certain level of jealousy involved for the women users who harass female influencers. Increased hatred by women users was observed when female influencers promoted their own product lines. The influencers were seen as having illegitimate careers supported by scamming their audiences (Duffy et al., 2022). This could also be seen as a disruption of gender norms as female business leaders are generally unrepresented in the United States (McLaughlin, 2012: Misra & Murray-Close, 2014)

Following the logic of gender norm violations, McLaughlin et al. (2012) found that women in authority positions endured more in-person workplace sexual harassment when compared to women in non-supervisory positions. This research was also supported by Folke et al., (2020) noting that women in male dominated professions are more likely to experience harassment when working at the supervisory level. Again, most influencers and social media users are female and societal constructed gender roles may be playing a part in why audiences treat female influencers negatively. Though the profession of influencing is female concentrated, their social media audience may not be. Considering that influencers are their own bosses, they are not "replacing" a male boss and disturbing any preconceived workplace hierarchies. However, they are their own bosses. Such independent professional success may trigger hegemonic philosophies in both male and female viewers that categorize women as belonging to the private sphere only and a female entrepreneur is seen as an anomaly.

Jane (2014) theorizes that the vitriolic online harassment observed to be aimed at women who are operating professionally in the online space is perpetuated by men who view female presence as an encroachment into traditionally male spaces. Folke et al., (2020) found this to be true in terrestrial workplaces. Academia and journalism are historically male dominated ventures. The fear and suffering invoked by such noxious rhetoric observed in the harassment of women in these professions may stem from societal subordination of femininity and is meant to dismiss and control women online by the very same harassment tactics employed within terrestrial spaces. This may hold true even if women comprise most social media users.

Therefore, women may be sacrificing their wellbeing to participate in the influence and control of culture online because they harassed while doing so (Adams, 2018). Influencers specifically are especially vulnerable to online harassment because their income earning potential is dependent on user-dependent metrics such as likes, comments and number of followers (Duffy & Hund, 2019). This observation is important because online harassment, especially of professional women as observed in research, causes them to change their behavior, speak out less or hide their true identities out of fear, entrenching a gender hierarchy into cyberspace that can disproportionately exclude women both socially and economically at times (Citron, 2009).

The technological, legal, and social structure of the internet allows gendered harassment online to flourish (Eckert, 2018). The systematic gender discrimination that is occurring online is not as tangibly prohibited by lawmakers or law enforcement when compared to workplace gendered harassment (Eckert, 2018). Even though men experience certain types of harassment online more often than women like name calling and physical threats, women are still more likely to experience online harassment overall (Pew Research Center, 2021). This is especially concerning for female influencers who may face career barriers from harassment that male influencers do not. This may present a barrier to women's advancement in society because the digital world is not truly separate from the tertiary world. Humans do not act online without acting offline also (Lazarus, 2019). Feminist theory suggest that gender inequality is likely the cause of the disproportionate harassment of women online, likely causing certain professionals, like influencers, to experience more negative impacts during their careers when compared to male influencers.

Routine Activity Theory

Internet use is becoming an irremovable element of daily existence causing humans and internet corporations to develop an extremely complex and interdependent relationship. Participation in online spaces is becoming a constant everyday activity for those in the developed world and even for some in developing countries. Online activity has become routine activity as people work, learn, communicate, and essentially live in the online world as much as they do in the terrestrial one. Though routine activity theory is a macro-level theory, it can be used to conceptualize online harassment as a crime problem. This paper is utilizing a macro-level theory and applying it to micro-level, individual victimization experiences. Where traditional routine activity theory and online harassment begin to diverge slightly is the realization that the perpetrator and the victim rarely interact in the "terrestrial" space as Cohen and Felson initially described in 1979. However, all the essential elements are still present. Law enforcement and social media platforms fail to act as capable guardians. There is a large and anonymous community of motivated offenders on social media that have access to suitable targets; people with public profiles and economically dependent influencers. Therefore, routine activity theory can be used to examine why harassment is happening online.

Social media platforms allow users to post content featuring their real existence often in real-time. A global network of complete strangers is therefore invited to view a person's life that would otherwise be private. Therefore, increased personal exposure, though online means, is becoming a routine activity, widening the pool of potential online harassment victims. In 2002, Spitzberg & Hoobler concluded that cyberstalking is correlated with the computer literacy of both the stalker and the victim. Because computers (including smartphones) are becoming an irreplaceable facet of modern life, computer literacy is rising among many people of all ages and in all parts of the world. Therefore, routine activity is putting more people at risk for

cyberstalking, harassment and a multitude of other types of victimization. There is also an ever-

growing pool of perpetrators that come along with increased internet use.

Cohen and Felson developed the routine activity theory in 1979 when the internet was

nonexistent. Routine activity theory is centered-around the assumption that everyday activities

present opportunities for direct predatory violations (Cohen & Felson, 1979), and predatory

violations are defined as when someone intentionally harms the person or property of another

(Cohen & Felson, 1979). A predatory violation in this context happens in a physical space at a

physical time in tandem with normal, non-predatory activities. Cohen and Felson theorize that a

change in American routine activities was causing an increase in certain types of crime like

home burglary due to more people being at work and fewer people (women) being present to

guard their homes. One could say that increasing technology use among Americans (and

worldwide) can certainly be labeled as a change in routine activities. Therefore, routine activity

theory can be used to frame the prevalence of online harassment in general. Measuring rates of

online harassment is beyond the scope of this theory. However, it does offer an applicable

analysis as to why harassment has become part of the user experience on social media.

When utilizing routine activity to explain online harassment, several options to decrease

victimization become apparent. If one element such as motivated offenders, available victims, or

lack of capable guardians is reduced, online harassment may decrease as a result. Instructing

victims to avoid the internet in order to protect themselves from online harassment, especially if

having an internet profile is their sole source of income, is unrealistic (Smith, 2018). Punishing

perpetrators for their harassment by removing them from social media is a violation of free

speech. Both of these options provide oversimplified solutions to the problem of online harassment and fail to address the potential economic, physiological and psychological impacts of victimization. Therefore, what remains is ensuring that social media corporations act as capable guardians by strengthening existing content moderation policies at the federal level.

Routine activity theory and feminist theory can usefully combine under the neoliberal internet. Social media platforms are profitable companies that operate in a neoliberal fashion. Their goal is user engagement no matter if it is positive or negative (Walter, 2022). The longer someone uses social media, the more advertising profit is derived from user engagement (Bhargava & Velasquez, 2021: Walter, 2022). Baer (2016) argues that a neoliberal internet empowers users with hegemonic qualities such as individual empowerment, emphasis on the rights of individual choice and an emphasis on the importance of their own thoughts. Essentially, users are empowered to exist online as they see fit, without the social constraints of the terrestrial world as they are one step removed behind a screen. In the case of influencer and harasser, both parties participate online to serve self-interests be it personal economic gain or self-expression that can result in psychosocial harm of others. Social media platforms profit either way. The individual and hegemonic neoliberal traits of the online world work to create motivated offenders and available victims. A lack of policy oversight allows for the absence of capable guardians. Gender inequality in the terrestrial world causes females online to experience increased harassment levels just as they do in the terrestrial world. Influencers are on social media to work and social media platforms are not obligated to protect them from harassment nor are they obligated to provide support when harassment impacts them emotionally, physically or economically. Thus, online harassment is a large-scale problem, rooted in policy failure and the social problems of the terrestrial world. These elements combine to create the perfect storm that social media corporations are not obligated to stop nor incentivized to stop because user engagement, be it good or bad, is profitable.

Current Study

It is known that women and professional women face harassment online (Adams, 2018: Jane 2018). Professionals like journalists and academics use social media to increase their career exposure. Most influencers are women (Duffy & Hund, 2019) and according to the literature, compared to men, are more likely to endure extreme abuse online such as cyber stalking and sexual harassment (Angus Reid, 2016). Gender inequality, like in the terrestrial American workplace, is also present in the online workspace. Eberspacher (2018) found that the physiological impacts on harassed female journalists included loss of sleep and appetite along with physiological impacts that include trauma, shame and stress. If female influencers, like other professions, are experiencing a disproportionate amount of negative attention (when compared to male influencers), there exist gendered barriers to economic success, free speech, and consequently, agency. Research is lacking when it comes to how online harassment impacts an influencer's (especially a female influencer's) ability to work and gain income on social media platforms.

This study has four distinct academic contributions. First, the economic, psychological and physiological impacts of online harassment have not been empirically tested together was one variable. It is unknown how these variables work in concert and if they are additive in the aggregate. Second, the combined impacts of online harassment have not been examined across genders. Third, the economic impacts of online harassment on social media have not been tested empirically for social media influencers. Fourth the economic impact of online harassment of social media influencers has not been examined across genders. To examine the criteria listed above, this study will address the following research questions:

RQ$_1$: Are there gender differences in online harassment?

H$_1$: Women will experience greater levels of harassment than men

RQ$_2$: What are the effects of online harassment?

H$_{2.1}$: An increase in online harassment will be associated with an increase in psychological impacts

H$_{2.2}$: An increase in online harassment will be associated with an increase in physiological impacts

H$_{2.3}$: An increase in online harassment will be associated with an increase in economic impacts

H$_{2.4}$: An increase in online harassment will be associated with an increase in combined impacts

RQ$_3$: Are there gender differences in combined impacts of online harassment?

H$_3$: Women who experience online harassment will experience greater combined economic, physiological and psychological effects than men

RQ$_4$: Does experiencing psychological and physiological effects make someone more likely to experience economic impacts?

H$_{4.1}$: Experiencing psychological and physiological effects will cause greater economic impacts.

RQ$_5$: Are there any factors associated with greater economic impacts for social media influencers?

$H_{5.1}$: Female social influencers will experience greater economic impact over male influencers

$H_{5.2}$: Social influencers experiencing more online harassment will experience higher levels of economic impact

Chapter Three: Methods

Sample

A mixed-method sampling technique was used to gather respondents. The author employed a combination of convenience sampling and snowball sampling. A self-administered survey was built in Qualtrics and posted as a live link to the author's Instagram, Facebook, Twitter and Reddit accounts. Data was collected from November 21, 2022, to January 23, 2023. Two public posts were made on the author's Instagram, Facebook and Twitter accounts inviting friends and followers to participate in the survey. Five posts were also made to the Reddit group r/samplesize, a group to specifically recruit survey respondents for academic research, under the author's account.

In total, 185 recruitment emails were sent inviting Instagram-based influencers to take the survey. Email invitations are likely the most visible way to contact influencers as their direct messages will likely be full of follower engagements such as story and poll responses, comments, and likes/emoji reactions from their audience. All influencers in the author's Instagram account were solicited to participate which amounted to 30 total. Influencer email addresses were gathered using Upfluence, a tool that provides a plethora of data on influencer accounts such as legal name, email, net worth, number of followers, follower engagement percentages, and more. Their free chrome extension allows the user to save the contact information of social media profiles on Instagram. The author chose to gather emails from Instagram only for the sake of time efficiency and, because of investments that Facebook (Meta), the owner of the platform, has made to further economic gain for influencers (Bradley, 2022). Upfluence can be used to gather data on Facebook (Meta) and YouTube as well.

From each of the original influencer accounts selected from the author's Instagram account, two accounts *that those selected influencers follow* were chosen arbitrarily and added to the contact list. This factorial pattern was repeated roughly twice to arrive at 185 influencer candidates to solicit with email messages. At times, the selected accounts did not have email addresses listed on their account pages, nor did they appear in the Upfluence software. If this situation occurred, another followed account was selected. Results of this study are not generalizable due to the inability to obtain a random sample. There is also a sampling bias as selections began with influencers that the author follows, which are comprised mainly of fitness and food related accounts. Limitations will be explored in further detail within chapter six.

The survey began with an informed consent section which stated that no identifying information will be collected from respondents such as names, social media profile handles, addresses, email addresses or phone numbers. The collection of IP addresses option was also disabled in Qualtrics prior to publishing the live survey. Therefore, all survey responses were downloaded from Qualtrics without any personal identifiers. Also, at the beginning of the survey was a link to Samaritans Hope[1], an organization that offers free emotional support at a time of crisis. Because the sampling methodology was designed to include international respondents, there are call, text or chat options available in over 240 languages. The conclusion of the survey displayed a link to a separate, secure survey where respondents could enter their email address in order to be entered into the gift card raffle. Four $25 Amazon gift cards were awarded to participants after the data was cleaned. Winning email addresses were chosen using a random number generator.

---

[1] Samaritan's Hope: https://samaritanshope.org/

Currently, there is no official operationalized definition of an influencer in sociological or criminological research. To be selected for the email list, influencer profiles had to be attached to a name and picture, not aliases. Their account content had to be centered around their identity as a content creator. Controls for this study attempted to examine someone's personal exposure online. Accounts that only share pictures of food or animals may not face the same levels of harassment as a person who shares pictures of their face or body. For example, mean comments about the cheesecake a person posted on their baking account may not induce as strong of a reaction as negative comments about the person's physical appearance. The survey in this study was written to study the impacts of harassment on people whose accounts represent their true selves. Influencers selected on Instagram had to have a minimum of 1,000 followers. The goal was to obtain a sample that had a minimum of 100 influencers and a minimum of 100 regular users for a total of 200 respondents.

On November 26, 2022, an influencer emailed back, reminding the author of Instagram's word blocking tool. The email stated that most influencers are continuously adding words to their blocked list, causing them to respond rarely or never to items on the harassment scale. Even though people may be leaving harassing comments or direct messages, they will not be visible. It was assumed by the author that the block feature was not widely used by influencers as it could potentially drive down post engagement levels. However, question 10 was added on 11/26 adding the block feature as a control variable.

The Presence of Bots in Online Research

Though social media is a cost-effective tool for recruiting survey participants, bots are an increasingly common threat to data quality. Bots are simply autonomous software applications that are programmed to perform interactions and tasks. One use case for a bot is taking online surveys many times in a row in order to increase the chances of winning a monetary prize. There is potential for bots to be deployed from server farms, which are large groups of hardware operating at the same location (Pozzar et al., 2020). Server farms can house a nearly infinite amount of virtual private servers, giving each bot a unique IP address (Pozzar et al., 2020) thereby making bot activity detection more difficult for researchers. One way around this is to use a survey instrument that records the physical location of respondents. Because server farms will register at identical or very similar latitudes and longitudes, a collection of surveys submitted at the same time from the same physical location are a likely indicator of bot induced fraudulence. Pozzar et al., (2020) lists several suggestions for avoiding and detecting bot activity on social media websites. Though not a complete list, some of these best practices include asking opened ended questions, asking questions with bait answers such as "where did you hear about this study" while listing one selection choice that is fake, record timestamps for survey start and submission, and include items with specific instructions like "choose the third answer choice." In their study, Pozzar et al., (2020) also filtered out response times that were too fast for a human to complete the survey.

A total of 1759 submissions were recorded at the closing of the survey. The data for both surveys was cleaned of bot submissions to the best of the author's ability. Because IP addresses and location identifiers had been disabled for the harassment survey (for anonymity and IRB approval), bot submissions were identified and removed using several methodologies. Bots can take surveys much faster than human respondents. Using a similar methodology proposed by Pozzar et al., (2020), the first step was filtering the data in SPSS by "duration in seconds" ascending. All harassment surveys that were 100% completed in 6 minutes and above (360 seconds) were filtered out and saved as a separate dataset. When manually tested, six minutes was the minimum amount of time that it would take for a human to complete the survey. The second bot identifier is submission timing. Bots will usually fill out many surveys, close together, in a noticeably short amount of time. The data was filtered by "end date" ascending. Any group of two or more responses that was submitted within the same day, hour and minute (with a + or - 1 second margin) were deleted. For example, a group of submissions at 00:12:59, 01:00:00, 01:00:01, 01:00:003 would be deleted. At the end of the process, a total of 708 survey responses remained.

Because the data collected from the email drawing survey was not anonymous, bot detection on this data was a simpler process. All data were sorted by IP addresses, ascending. All data submitted by the same IP addresses were deleted as this is likely to be bot activity or a human respondent cheating and entering their email multiple times for an increased chance of winning the gift card drawing. Next, bots can work on multiple devices (with different IP addresses) in the same location (Pozzar et al., 2020). The data was next sorted into location latitude, ascending. All duplicates of matching latitude and longitude were deleted as they were likely from a server farm. After cleaning, 442 responses remained. Though this is less than the 708 total harassment survey responses, it is likely that not all respondents from the initial survey decided to enter the drawing. It could also be likely that bots would generate more responses to the email drawing survey than the initial survey, especially if they are programmed to seek monetary gain. Higher numbers of bot responses results in a greater number of these responses to be deleted. Four winners were selected using a random number generator and sent a digital amazon gift card directly from the author's Amazon account. The Northern Arizona University Investigating Difference fund[2] issued the $100 as a grant to fund respondent compensation in this study.

---

[2] Investigating difference fund: https://nau.edu/criminology-and-criminal-justice/graduate-financial-aid/

Measures

Dependent Variables

 Online Harassment. Wilson et al. (2022) created a scale to operationalize the study of Cyberstalking in research. Since all cyberstalking behaviors are under the umbrella of online harassment, this scale includes 24 questions about unwanted behaviors such as threats, unwanted sexual images, and doxing[3]. There were also a few questions about disparaging comments made about the person's appearances, gender or intellect as these items were reported as common forms of harassment in other areas of literature. Cronbach's alpha is (α=0.968) indicating a high level of consistency between scale items. Respondents will be asked how often they experience the listed behaviors within an average week. If a respondent clicks "never" to all harassment criteria, skip logic will take them to the end of the survey to avoid answer questions on the other impact scales. The prompts for the impact scales following the harassment scale are phrased *"After experiencing the online harassment behaviors mentioned previously, often do you feel the following?* If the respondent had not experienced any of the harassment behaviors mentioned in the Wilson et al. (2022) scale, they would not be able to answer any questions on the impact scales. Also, they would likely stop taking the survey, resulting in a loss of their demographic data which appeared at the end.

 Psychological Subscale: Psychological effects will be measured using select items from the "Emotional Symptoms" scale from Begotti & Maran (2019) in composite with two additions from Villacampos & Pujols, (2018). Begotti & Maran (2019) included items such as sadness, fear, anger, agoraphobia, loss of self-esteem and laxative use. Laxative use was moved to the emotional impacts scale changed to substance use for the purposes of this study as a multitude of different

---

[3] Doxing is the publishing of a person's private information online without their consent (Wilson et al., 2022)

purchasable substances could be used to cope with the emotional impacts of online harassment. Difficulty concentrating and depression were added to this scale from Villacampa & Pujols, (2018). Difficulty concentrating is an intrusive mental symptom that can negatively impact victims of online harassment. Hassan et al. (2018) list "loss of sleep, low self-esteem, anxiety and depression" as psychological effects and so do Villacampa & Pujols (2018). Depression was measured by Begotti & Maran (2019) based on respondent scores to the emotional symptoms scale. This study was not measuring depression that way and asked explicitly about depression for clarity of experience. The scale listed a high Cronbach's alpha (α=0.938) indicating a high level of consistency between scale items. Please refer to appendix D, under "psychological impact scales" for the full list of items included in the scale

Physiological Subscale: As previously mentioned, Begotti & Maran (2019) created a "physical" symptoms scale to assess the physical impacts of cyberstalking victimization. Attributes include weight change, sleep disorders, vomiting, and others. Following the logic of Villacampa & Pujols (2018), anxiety attacks was moved from Begotti & Maran's (2019) physical symptoms scale onto the "psychological impacts" for consistency. The Cronbach's alpha for the composite scale was also high (α=0.923), indicating a high level of consistency between scale items. See Appendix D under "physiological impacts scale" for the full list of items included in the scale.

Economic Subscale: The economic subscale for this study was generated using a combination of items from a multitude of studies. To avoid developing multiple scales and in an effort to make one, standardized scale, a single economic impact scale was developed for users and influencers. Maple et al. (2011) conducted a study of cyberstalking victimization in the UK. They separated financial consequences and employment consequences into separate categories.

This study combined elements from Maple et al. (2011) under one "economic impacts scale." Attributes include changing the way that you work, paying for therapy and security measures and declining work performance. Hassan et al. (2018) list "account closure, loss of brand deal" as specific economic impacts for influencers and they were included on the economic impact scale. Begotti et al., (2019) listed protective mechanisms taken by respondents such as a decrease in internet use and, purchase of a weapon. These items cost money and were included on the scale. Because of Wilson et al.'s (2022) mention of online stalking transitioning to offline stalking, an item about moving housing locations was added from Villacampa & Pujol's (2018) stalking impacts scale. They also included the purchasing of a weapon. Cronbach's alpha for this scale is ($\alpha=0.898$) indicating a high level of consistency between scale items. For the full list of items included in the scale, see Appendix C under "Economic impacts."

Combined Impacts of Harassment. Three sub-scales that measure the psychological, economic and physiological impacts that may arise from experiencing online harassment. The distinctive measure between psychological impacts and physiological impacts is not standardized in research. Begotti & Maran (2019) separate impacts into "physical symptoms" and "emotional symptoms." This methodology will be followed by using their scales, but "emotional symptoms" will be labeled as "psychological symptoms" and "physical symptoms" will be labeled as physiological symptoms. Cronbach's alpha is ($\alpha=0.963$) indicating a high level of consistency between scale items.

Independent Variables

Online Harassment. Wilson et al. (2022) created a scale to operationalize the study of Cyberstalking in research. Since all cyberstalking behaviors are under the umbrella of online harassment, this scale includes 24 questions about unwanted behaviors such as threats, unwanted sexual images, and doxing[4]. There were also a few questions about disparaging comments made about the person's appearances, gender or intellect as these items were reported as common forms of harassment in other areas of literature. Cronbach's alpha is (α=0.968) indicating a high level of consistency between scale items. Respondents will be asked how often they experience the listed behaviors within an average week. If a respondent clicks "never" to all harassment criteria, skip logic will take them to the end of the survey. The prompts for the impact scales following the harassment scale are phrased *"After experiencing the online harassment behaviors mentioned previously, often do you feel the following?* If the respondent had not experienced any of the harassment behaviors mentioned in the Wilson et al. (2022) scale, they would not be able to answer any questions on the impact scales. Also, they would likely stop taking the survey, resulting in a loss of their demographic data which appeared at the end.

Gender. Gender is measured by the question *"with which gender do you identify."* Attributes listed are "Woman, Man, Transgender woman, Transgender man, Non-binary, Other." Henry & Powell (2016) and Veletsianos et al. (2018) both found that women experience gendered harassment online more often than men, yet Fissel & Reyns (2019) reported that the average female internet user is not more likely to experience harassment online. Pew Research Center (2021) concluded in their survey that men are more likely experience harassment behaviors generally, while women are more likely to experience "severe" harassment that is sexual and hateful. Feminist theory predicts that online harassment is the result of gender inequality that has the potential to disadvantage women in the online workspace created by social media platforms. For data analysis purposes, gender was dichotomized into the categories of "women" (including trans women) and "men" (including trans men) because this is how they identify and present themselves.

---

[4] Doxing is the publishing of a person's private information online without their consent (Wilson et al., 2022)

Non-binary and other were listed as system missing since there were only 3 respondents in each category.

Psychological Subscale: Psychological effects will be measured using select items from the "Emotional Symptoms" scale from Begotti & Maran (2019) with two additions from Villacampos & Pujols, (2018). Begotti & Maran (2019) included items such as sadness, fear, anger, agoraphobia, loss of self-esteem and laxative use. Laxative use was moved to the emotional impacts scale changed to substance use for the purposes of this study as a multitude of different purchasable substances could be used to cope with the emotional impacts of online harassment. Difficulty concentrating and depression were added to this scale from Villacampa & Pujols, (2018). Difficulty concentrating is an intrusive mental symptom that can negatively impact victims of online harassment. Hassan et al. (2018) list "loss of sleep, low self-esteem, anxiety and depression" as psychological effects and so do Villacampa & Pujols (2018). Depression was measured by Begotti & Maran (2019) based on respondent scores to the emotional symptoms scale. This study was not measuring depression that way and asked explicitly about depression for clarity of experience. The scale listed a high Cronbach's alpha ($\alpha=0.938$) indicating a high level of consistency between scale items. Please refer to appendix D, under "psychological impact scales" for the full list of items included in the scale.

Physiological Subscale: As previously mentioned, Begotti & Maran (2019) created a "physical" symptoms scale to assess the physical impacts of cyberstalking victimization. Attributes include weight change, sleep disorders, vomiting, and others. Anxiety attacks was moved from the physical symptoms scale onto the "psychological impacts" scale for this study as anxiety attacks are primarily a mental symptom associated with anxiety. Villacampa & Pujols (2018) also included "panic attacks" as a psychological symptom. Cronbach's alpha for this scale was also high (α=0.923), indicating a high level of consistency between scale items. See Appendix E under "physiological impacts scale" for the full list of items included in the scale.

Control Variables

Because one of the assumptions of Ordinary Least Squares regression is that predictor variables are either continuous or dichotomous (Berry, 1993), all variables measured at the ordinal level were re-coded into dichotomous dummy variables. All continuous variables were not recoded.

Influencer status. Understanding influencer status is important as it determines how dependent someone is on their social media status for income. As previously mentioned, Fissel & Reyns (2019) found that the average woman using social media is not more likely to experience harassment. This may be different for influencers in general, especially female influencers as influencers are more exposed and active online. Influencer status is measured by the question *"Which option best describes the way that you use social media?* Attributes include Influencer (50% of income + 1,000 or more followers on a single platform), Aspiring influencer (0-49% of income made on social media and/or less than 1000 followers on a single platform), Previously aspired to be an influencer but not anymore, have never attempted to be an influencer." This variable was dichotomized into a comparison group which included only influencers labeled "yes" and a reference group labeled "no" for those who are not actually an influencer. Influencers are economically dependent on social media engagement and are likely creating content for a public audience. This increases their exposure online which may make them more vulnerable to harassment.

Reading Comments. This variable was measured by asking respondents: *"In an average week, how often do you read the comments on your posts?"* Answer choices were presented on a

Likert scale from always to never. Responses were dichotomized in a comparison group labeled "often" which included always and often and a reference group containing all other attributes. If a respondent is being harassed in their comments but does not read them, they may report harassment behaviors occurring less often. On the contrary, if a respondent reads their comments regularly, they may report harassment behaviors as occurring more often.

Time on social media. This variable was measured by asking respondents, *"on average, how much time do you spend on social media each day?* Answer choices included under one hour, 1-3 hours, 4-6 hours and 6+ hours. Answers were dichotomized into "0-3 hours" and "4+ hours." The longer a respondent spends on social media, the more likely they are to encounter harassing behaviors from others.

Face Content. Face content asked *"How often do you share content (stories, posts etc.) that has your face in it?* Response choices were presented on a Likert scale from *Always to Never*. Responses were dichotomized by grouping "always" & "often" into the comparison group labeled "Often" and "sometimes, rarely, and never" grouped into a reference category and labeled as "Not often." The more that a respondent shares content with their face in view, the more opportunity there is for their audience to comment on their personal appearance thereby increasing harassment exposure, so the 2 response categories that indicated more frequent posting of face content was grouped together and compared to those who did not post content as frequently.

Active sponsorship. Having an active sponsorship determines a respondent's economic dependence on social media platform performance. Therefore, it may impact how a person will experience and respond to harassment behaviors. To generate an income from social media, a person could continue to build a follower base despite dealing with high levels of harassment. Influencers and aspiring influencers only were shown this question. The attributes are *"Do you* *have an active sponsorship?"* with answer choices of "yes" or "no" which naturally dichotomized the variable.

Location. Internet access varies throughout the world. Therefore, social media harassment experiences are likely to be more commonplace in locations where social media access is attainable. Location will be measured by the question *"Where do you currently live?"* with the answer choices of Asia, Africa, North America, South America, Europe, Australia, Caribbean Islands, Pacific Islands, other. Antarctica has been omitted as no formal country exists there. A slight majority of the sample was from North America and no other continents had enough responses to warrant being the comparison category, so this variable was dichotomized into North America and other.

Block feature. Instagram, Facebook (Meta) and YouTube allow users to add words or phrases to a blocked list. So, if a user is being harassed while employing this tool, they may not see most of the degrading comments as they keep adding to their blocked list. This will likely impact how a person will score on the harassment scale. Block feature use will be measured with the question *"Some social media platforms allow users to block certain words or phrases from appearing in your direct messages and public comments. Which way best describes how you use this blocking feature?"* Answer choices include: "I have heard of this feature and use it regularly, I have heard of this feature and I occasionally add new words to my blocked list, I have heard of this feature, but I don't use it, I have never heard of this feature, but I would like to use it, I have never heard of this feature, and I would not be interested in using it." For analysis, this variable was dichotomized into those who use the feature and those who do not. If respondents utilize the block feature, they may experience less harassment as certain comments with specified words or phrases would not be visible to them.

Content type. Content type will be included as a control as it could influence the level of harassment that a user experiences. The question measuring content type asked *"What best describes the majority of the content you post?"* Response categories included Health/fitness, Fashion/beauty, Cooking/Food, Political, Professional, Parenting/Family, Hobby based, Academic/educational, personal, other." This variable was dichotomized into "Fashion/beauty/health fitness" as the comparison category and all others were coded into the reference group Having an account strictly focused on appearance-based criteria such as fashion/beauty or health/fitness may cause an increase in harassment levels due to giving other users the opportunity to comment on appearance. Duffy & Hund (2019) found that female influencers are harassed by female users because they were seen to be promoting unrealistic expectations for average women. This indicates that there may be potential resentment towards respondents who post this type of content, potentially exposing them to increased levels of harassment. Therefore, the two categories most likely to evoke criticism from others were used for the comparison category.

Gender. Gender is measured by the question "with which gender do you identify." Attributes listed are "Woman, Man, Transgender woman, Transgender man, Non-binary, Other." Henry & Powell (2016) and Veletsianos et al. (2018) both found that women experience gendered harassment online more often than men, yet Fissel & Reyns (2019) reported that the average female internet user is not more likely to experience harassment online. Pew Research Center (2021) concluded in their survey that men are more likely experience harassment behaviors generally, while women are more likely to experience "severe" harassment that is sexual and hateful. Feminist theory predicts that online harassment is the result of gender inequality that has the potential to disadvantage women in the online workspace created by social media platforms. For data analysis purposes, gender was dichotomized into the categories of "women" (including trans women) and "men" (including trans men) as they comprised most of the sample. Non-binary and other were listed as system missing as the population size for these categories was 3.

Analysis

Ordinary Least Squares (OLS) regression was the analytic technique used for all models in this study. This method assumes that the dependent variable is continuous while the independent variables can be continuous or dichotomous (Berry, 1993). Because all dependent variables in this study are continuous scales, OLS regression is a good choice over other types of regression, such as logistic regression, that do not assume a continuous dependent variable.

To test the first hypothesis that women would experience greater levels of harassment than men, a model was run with the entire sample. Controls such as location, content type, using the block feature, posting face content, time on social media and active sponsorship were added as they may impact the level of harassment experienced by respondents.

Because the prompt for all impact scales were prefaced with the words "*After experiencing the online harassment behaviors mentioned previously...*" the impact scales were irrelevant to respondents who had not been harassed and therefore would be unable to answer the impact questions. If respondents stated that they had never been harassed, they were skipped to the end and not shown the impact scales. Therefore, in order to include only relevant responses and avoid missing data, a filtered dataset, "Harassed Only," was created, containing only those who were harassed and shown the impact questions. Utilizing the entire sample would include too many respondents that had not been harassed and therefore not shown the impact scales, which would have resulted in a large amount of missing data. Further, in order to compare the effects of harassment on the three types of impact and the combined impact (hypotheses 2.1-2.4) all controls were kept the same across all models for the sake of comparison. These include, location, content type, use of the block feature, face content, time spent in social media and influencer status were added as controls because they may influence how much harassment respondents will report.

To test hypothesis 3.1 that women will experience greater combined impacts, a model was run using the Harassed Only dataset. Location, content type, use of the block feature, face content, time spent in social media and influencer status were added as controls because they may influence how much harassment respondents will face.

To test hypothesis 4.1 that experiencing psychological and physiological effects will cause greater economic impacts, a model was run using a filtered dataset of only harassed respondents. Utilizing the entire sample would include too many respondents who had not experienced harassment, resulting in a large amount of missing data. Gender, location, content type, reding comments, time on social media, face content and block feature were used as controls as they may influence the level of harassment that respondents may encounter. Active sponsorship was used instead of influencer status to measure economic vulnerability more directly.

To test hypothesis 5.1 that female social influencers will experience greater economic impact over male influencers and hypothesis 5.2 that social influencers experiencing more online harassment will experience higher levels of economic impacts, a model was run using a filtered dataset of only influencers who had experienced harassment. Location, content type, use of the block feature, face content, time spent in social media and influencer status were added as controls because they may influence how much harassment respondents will face.

Chapter Four: Results

Descriptives

Table 1 presents the descriptive data for all variables in the models. After bot response

elimination, 708 valid responses remained in total.

This study did not include many demographic variables as they were not addressed in the

research questions or hypotheses. Overall, the majority of the sample were heterosexual (80%),

and 20% identified as homosexual. The youngest respondent was 18 years old and the oldest was

64 years old with 75% were between the ages of 18-32, and 16% were between the ages of 33-

40, and the remaining 9% were over the age of 40. A more detailed description of sample

characteristics for all variables in the models can be found in Table 1.

For continuous variables, respondents experienced a relatively high amount of

harassment as a mean of 76.94 is higher than the average of the minimum and maximum listed.

Regarding impacts, of the respondents who had experienced harassment behaviors, combined

impacts were observed with no individual impact scales listing a disproportionately high mean.

Table 1.

Descriptive Statistics of Sample

	N	Range	Minimum	Maximum	Mean	Std. Dev
Combined Impacts Scale	325	116	47	163	115.81	24.285
Psychological Impact Scale	348	45	20	65	46.38	10.532
Physiological Impact Scale	347	37	13	50	36.86	8.054
Economic Impact Scale	360	40	8	48	32.02	8.312
Harassment Scale	638	84	21	105	76.94	18.264
Time Spent (1= 4+ Hrs)	701	1	0	1	0.50	0.500
Active Sponsorship (1= Yes)	569	1	0	1	0.23	0.420
Gender (1= Woman)	688	1	0	1	0.46	0.499
Content Type (1= Health/Beauty)	362	1	0	1	0.34	0.473
Block Feature (1= Yes)	708	1	0	1	0.66	0.470
Influencer or Aspiring (1= Yes)	698	1	0	1	0.44	0.497
Read Comments (1= Often)	708	1	0	1	0.77	0.424
Face Content (1= Often)	708	1	0	1	0.84	0.368
Location (1= North America)	708	1	0	1	0.55	0.498

For variables that are dichotomous, the mean can be read as the percentage of the sample that were in the one category. Thus, 77% of the respondents read their comments, and a majority of respondents, 84%, post content that has their face in it. Most respondents were from North America, but about 45% were from various other continents such as Europe, Africa, and Asia. Women comprised 46% of the sample and men comprised 54%, so there were a slight majority of men. Roughly 44% of the total sample stated that they are an influencer with only 23% of respondents reported having an active sponsorship (see Table 1).

Outcomes

Research Question 1: Are there gender differences in online harassment?

The results of the OLS regression model testing the hypothesis that women would experience more harassment than men experience are shown in Table 2. The model is statistically significant overall (F=2.279, p.=.009). and can explain 23% of the variance in harassment scores (R^2=.0.23). Because gender is not significant, the first hypothesis, that women would experience greater harassment than men do is not supported. Location was found to have a significant negative relationship to harassment (B=-2.862, p.=0.001). Respondents are 2.862 times *less* likely to experience harassment if they are located in North America. No other controls in the model are significant. (See Table 2).

Table 2.

OLS Model Predicting the Relationship Between Gender and Harassment (N=708)

	Unstandardized Coefficient		Standardized Coefficient		
	B	(s.e)	β	t	p.
(Constant)	80.448	4.045		19.890	<.001
Gender (1= Woman)	-2.941	1.694	-0.079	-1.736	0.083
Location (1= North America)	-2.862	0.878	-0.146	-3.262	**0.001**
Content Type (1=Health/ Beauty)	-0.335	1.680	-0.009	-0.199	0.842
Block Feature (1= Yes)	0.730	1.912	0.017	0.382	0.703
Face Content (1= Often)	-1.597	1.755	-0.042	-0.910	0.363
Time on Social Media (1= 4+ hrs)	-2.128	1.633	-0.057	-1.303	0.193
Active Sponsorship (1=Yes)	2.429	1.981	0.055	1.226	0.221

Model R^2= 0.23, df=7, F=2.279, p.=0.09

Research Question 2: What are the effects of online harassment?

The results of the OLS regression testing the hypothesis that an increase in online harassment will be associated with an increase in psychological impacts are reported in Table 3. The model overall is statistically significant (F=56.358, p=<.001) and can explain about 59% of the variance in the scores on the psychological impact scale (R^2=.590). As hypothesized, there was a statistically significant positive relationship between harassment and psychological impacts (B=0.463, p.=<.001). Therefore, hypothesis 2.1 that an increase in online harassment would be associated with an increase in psychological impacts is supported. Each additional point on the harassment scale, indicating greater harassment, is associated with a 0.463 increase in psychological impacts. Therefore, the higher a respondent scores on the harassment scale, the more psychological impacts they are likely to experience.

There was also a significant negative effect for gender (B= -1.806, p. =0.026) in this model. Women and transwomen are 1.806 times *less* likely to experience psychological impacts. Location was also statistically significant (B=3.767 p.= <.001), with respondents located in

North America being 3.767 times more likely to experience psychological impact. No other controls were significant (see Table 3).

Table 3.
OLS Regression Model Predicting Psychological Impacts (N=362)

	Unstandardized Coefficient		Standardized Coefficient		
	B	(s.e)	β	t	p.
(Constant)	8.758	2.259		3.876	<.001
Harassment Scale	0.463	0.024	0.734	19.358	**<.001**
Gender (1= Woman)	-1.806	0.810	-0.086	-2.230	**0.026**
Location (1= North America)	3.767	0.837	0.167	4.499	**<.001**
Content Type (1=Health/ Beauty)	-1.397	0.856	-0.064	-1.631	0.104
Block Feature (1= Yes)	1.551	0.890	0.068	1.743	0.082
Face Content (1= Often)	0.091	0.845	0.004	0.108	0.914
Time on Social Media (1= 4+ hrs)	-1.052	0.837	-0.050	-1.257	0.210
Influencer Status (1=Yes)	0.497	0.805	0.023	0.617	0.538

Model R^2=.590, df= 8, F=56.358, p= <.001

The results of the OLS regression model testing the hypothesis that an increase in harassment would be associated with an increase in physiological impacts is shown in Table 4. The model is statistically significant overall (F=38.480 p.=<.001) and can explain about 50% of the variance in harassment scores (R^2=.503). As hypothesized, there was a statistically significant positive relationship between harassment and physiological impacts (B=0.330, p.= <.001). Therefore, hypothesis 2.2 that harassment would be associated with physiological impacts is supported. Each point on the harassment scale, indicating greater harassment, is associated with a 0.33 increase in physiological impacts. The more harassment that respondents report on the harassment scale, the more physiological impacts they will likely experience. Location was also significant (B=2.325, p.= 0.001) in this model. Respondents located in North America are 2.325 times more likely to experience physiological impacts. No other variables were significant (see Table 4).

Table 4.

OLS Regression Model Predicting Physiological Impacts (N=362)

	Unstandardized Coefficient		Standardized Coefficient		
	B	(s.e)	β	t	p.
(Constant)	10.640	1.939		5.488	<.001
Harassment Scale	0.330	0.020	0.679	16.216	**<.001**
Gender (1= Woman)	-0.798	0.684	-0.049	-1.166	0.244
Location (1= North America)	2.325	0.702	0.136	3.310	**0.001**
Content Type (1=Health/ Beauty)	-0.843	0.720	-0.050	-1.170	0.243
Block Feature (1= Yes)	0.022	0.747	0.001	0.029	0.977
Face Content (1= Often)	-0.211	0.710	-0.013	-0.297	0.767
Time on Social Media (1= 4+ hrs)	-0.657	0.705	-0.040	-0.931	0.353
Influencer Status (1=Influencer)	0.449	0.681	0.028	0.660	0.510

R^2=.503, df=8, F=38.480, p= <.001

The results of the OLS regression testing the hypothesis that an increase in online harassment will be associated with an increase in economic impacts is shown in Table 5. The model is statistically significant overall (F=24.368, p.=<.001) and can explain 37% of the variance in harassment scores (R^2=.370). As hypothesized, there was a statistically significant positive relationship between harassment and economic impacts (B=0.287, p. =<.001) therefore, hypothesis 2.3 that an increase in harassment would be associated with an increase in economic impacts is supported. Each point on the harassment scale indicating greater harassment is associated with a 0.287 increase in economic impacts. The higher that respondents score on the harassment scale, the more economic impacts they are likely to experience. The block feature was also negatively significant (B= 1.772, p. = 0.038) in this model. Respondents who utilize the block feature are 1.772 times *less* likely to experience economic impacts. No other variables were significant (see Table 5).

Table 5.

OLS Model Predicting Economic Impact (N=362)

	Unstandardized Coefficient		Standardized Coefficient		
	B	(s.e)	β	t	p.
(Constant)	11.327	2.174		5.209	<.001
Harassment Scale	0.287	0.023	0.570	12.346	**<.001**
Gender (1= Woman)	-0.461	0.773	-0.028	-0.596	0.552
Location (1= North America)	1.167	0.792	0.067	1.473	0.142
Content Type (1=Health/ Beauty)	-0.460	0.822	-0.027	-0.560	0.576
Block Feature (1= Yes)	-1.772	0.849	-0.100	-2.086	**0.038**
Face Content (1= Often)	-1.369	0.813	-0.082	-1.685	0.093
Time on Social Media (1= 4+ hrs)	0.797	0.803	0.048	0.992	0.322
Influencer Status (1=Yes)	-1.358	0.778	-0.081	-1.746	0.082

R^2=0.370, df=8, F=24.368, p= <.001

Research Question 2 & Research Question 3: Are there gender differences in combined impacts of online harassment?

The results of the OLS regression model testing the hypotheses that greater levels of harassment would be associated with greater combined impacts and that women will experience greater combined impacts is shown in Table 6. The model is statistically significant overall (F=55.335, p.=<.001) and can explain 59% of the variance in harassment scores (R^2=0.597). As hypothesized, there was a statistically significant positive relationship between harassment and combined impacts (B=1.113, p. =<.001) in this model, therefore hypothesis 2.4 is supported. Each point on the harassment scale, indicating greater harassment is associated with a 1.113 increase in combined impacts. The higher a respondent scores on the harassment scale, the greater combined impacts they are likely to experience. Because gender is insignificant, hypothesis 3.1 that women will experience greater combined impacts is not supported. Location was also significant (B=7.544, p.= <.001) in this model. Respondents located in North America are 7.544 times more likely to experience combined impacts. No other variables were significant (see Table 6).

Table 6.

OLS Regression Model Predicting Combined Impacts of Harassment (N=362)

	Unstandardized Coefficient		Standardized Coefficient		
	B	(s.e)	β	t	p.
(Constant)	26.979	5.488		4.916	<.001
Harassment Scale	1.113	0.057	0.751	19.429	**<.001**
Gender (1= Woman)	-2.700	1.909	-0.055	-1.415	0.158
Location (1= North America)	7.544	1.994	0.142	3.783	**<.001**
Content Type (1=Health/ Beauty)	-2.885	2.004	-0.057	-1.440	0.151
Block Feature (1= Yes)	0.215	2.098	0.004	0.102	0.918
Face Content (1= Often)	-0.890	1.979	-0.018	-0.450	0.653
Time on Social Media (1= 4+ hrs)	-0.783	1.994	-0.016	-0.393	0.695
Influencer Status (1=Yes)	0.152	1.909	0.003	0.080	0.937

R^2= .597, df=8, F=55.335, p= <.001

Research Question 4: **Does experiencing psychological and physiological effects make someone more likely to experience economic impacts?**

The results of the OLS regression model testing the hypothesis that experiencing

psychological and physiological effects will cause greater economic impacts is shown in Table 7.

The model is statistically significant overall (F=28.6, p.=<.001) and can explain 54% of the

variance in harassment scores (R^2=0.545). There was a small but statistically significant effect of

harassment on economic impact (B=0.078, p.=0.021). Each additional point on the harassment

scale, indicating greater harassment, is associated with a 0.07 increase in economic impacts.

Additionally, psychological impacts had a significant effect on economic impacts (B=0.174,

p.=0.023). Each additional point on the psychological scale, indicating greater psychological

impact, is associated with a 0.17 increase in economic impacts. Also, physiological impacts had

a significant effect on economic impacts (B=0.369, p.= <.001). Each point on the physiological

scale, indicating an increase in psychological impacts, is associated with a 0.36 increase in

economic impacts. The higher that respondents score on the psychological and physiological

impact scales, the greater economic impacts they are likely to experience. Therefore, hypothesis

4.1 that experiencing psychological and physiological effects makes someone more likely to experience economic impacts is supported. Finally, having an active sponsorship makes someone 1.8 times more likely to experience economic impacts.

The model for hypothesis 4.1 presents an issue of high collinearity. Berry & Feldman (1985) state that unless there is perfect collinearity, or a coefficient of +/- 1.0, the assumptions of a regression model are not invalidated. A VIF value above 5.0 is cause for concern, but a VIF value above 10 indicates a collinearity problem (Menard, 2001). The psychological impact scale VIF in this model is 5.7, which implies that there is a high correlation with another independent variable in the model. When examining the collinearity diagnostics, the psychological subscale has a value of 0.94 and the physiological subscale has a value of 0.74. O'Brien (2007) suggests removing highly correlated variables from the model in order to remedy a situation of collinearity but that is not possible in this case as psychological and physiological impacts are both being tested in the hypothesis. Though these two variables appear to be highly correlated, there is an explanation.

The scales used in this research are from Begotti et al., (2022) which analyzed the impacts of online harassment using "physical symptoms" and "emotional symptoms" scales that they developed. The author of this study decided to move anxiety attacks from the physical symptoms scale onto the "psychological impacts" scale. Though the change was minor, these scales are related and therefore it is reasonable that these two scales would be so highly correlated. (See Table 7)

Table 7.

OLS Regression Model Measuring Economic Impacts (N=362)

	Unstandardized Coefficient		Standardized Coefficient		
	B	(s.e)	β	t	p.
(Constant)	2.702	2.332		1.159	0.248
Harassment Scale	0.078	0.034	0.160	2.321	**0.021**
Psychological Impact Scale	0.174	0.076	0.232	2.289	**0.023**
Physiological Impact Scale	0.369	0.087	0.378	4.252	**<.001**
Gender (1= Woman)	-0.117	0.764	-0.007	-0.153	0.879
Active Sponsorship (1=Yes)	1.825	0.760	0.105	2.402	**0.017**
Location (1= North America)	-0.566	0.829	-0.032	-0.683	0.495
Content Type (1=Health/ Beauty)	-0.729	0.756	-0.044	-0.964	0.336
Read Comments (1= Often)	1.134	0.963	0.060	1.177	0.240
Time on Social Media (1= 4+ hrs)	0.941	0.773	0.057	1.217	0.225
Face Content (1= Often)	-1.375	0.784	-0.083	-1.755	0.081
Block Feature (1= Yes)	-1.248	0.844	-0.067	-1.478	0.141

R^2= .545, df=11, F=28.6, p= <.001

Research Question 5: Are There Any Factors Associated with Greater Economic Impacts for Social Media Influencers?

The results of the OLS regression model testing the hypotheses that female social

influencers will experience greater economic impact over male influencers and that social

influencers experiencing more online harassment will experience higher levels of economic

impacts is shown in Table 8. The model is statistically significant overall (F=6.62, p.= <.001)

and can explain 24% of the variance in harassment scores (R^2=0.242). Because gender was not

significant, hypothesis 5.1 that that women would experience more economic impacts is not

supported. Because harassment was significant (B=0.198. p.= <.001) hypothesis 5.2 that social

influencers who experience online harassment will experience higher levels of economic impacts

is supported. Each additional point on the harassment scale, indicating greater harassment, is

associated with a 0.19 increase in economic impacts. Influencers who experience higher levels of

harassment are more likely to experience economic impacts. No other variables were significant

(See Table 8).

Table 8.

OLS Regression Model 3, Measuring Economic Impacts on Social Influencers (N=159)

	Unstandardized Coefficient		Standardized Coefficient		
	B	(s.e)	β	t	p.
(Constant)	16.148	3.536		4.566	<.001
Harassment Scale	0.198	0.042	0.398	4.724	**<.001**
Gender (1= Woman)	-2.165	1.460	-0.122	-1.482	0.141
Location (1= North America)	2.176	1.509	0.112	1.442	0.152
Content Type (1= Health/ Fashion)	-0.528	1.468	-0.029	-0.359	0.720
Read Comments (1=Often)	1.008	1.806	0.051	0.558	0.578
Time on social media (1=4+ hrs)	1.864	1.737	0.099	1.073	0.285
Face Content (1=Often)	-0.653	1.590	-0.035	-0.411	0.682
Block Feature (1= Yes)	-2.459	1.680	-0.124	-1.464	0.146

Model R^2=.242, F=6.62, df=8, p.= <.001

Chapter Five: Discussion & Conclusion

This chapter will discuss the key findings of this research based on the analyses provided in the previous chapter. Additionally, this chapter highlights the limitations of this research project, presents policy implications and provides recommendations for future research.

This study adds to the literature by empirically testing the combined impacts of online harassment psychological, physiological and economic, as a combined impact. It is known from other research that online harassment has psychological, physiological and economic impacts when examined individually (Begotti & Maran 2019: Hassan et al., 2018: Maple et al., 2011). However, it is unknown how these impacts behave in concert. This study has added to existing literature by testing the combined impacts of online harassment on users across genders. Finally, this study also adds to existing literature by examining the economic impacts that online harassment has on influencers specifically while examining this effect across genders.

Harassment

This study adds to the literature by highlighting that online harassment does have combined negative psychological, physiological and economic impacts. When impacts are examined in concert, the influence of harassment is stronger. Harassment was found to be significant in every model of this study where it was used as an independent variable, indicating that experiencing harassment has negative impacts for social media users and influencers. This aligns with the cyberstalking studies mentioned in the literature review (Begotti & Maran, 2019: Villacampa & Pujols, 2018: Maple et al., 2011). Most importantly, the impact of harassment was strongest when the combined effects were examined together as a single variable. Psychological, physiological and economic impacts of online harassment present a stronger harassment score for those who are victimized, when examined in concert. Negative treatment online has a multitude of consequences for users offline. Routine activity theory predicts that a lack of capable guardians, available victims and motivated offenders enable crime. The negative impacts of online harassment can certainly be labeled as a social harm and can be labeled as a crime in the United States because all 50 states have anti-stalking laws (Smith, 2018). However, social media corporations are not legally required to take steps that reduce these consequences for their users. The "good-faith" loophole in Section 230 of the Communications Decency Act does not create a measurable standard for corporations to aspire to when it comes to liability or the removal of harmful content on their sites (Spiccia, 2013). The United States government has allowed social media corporations to become incapable guardians to their users. Therefore, harassing comments are likely a permanent facet of social media participation.

Gender

When testing the hypothesis that an increase in online harassment will be associated with an increase in psychological impacts, gender was found to be associated with a decrease in psychological impacts. In all other models, gender is insignificant. Despite the body of research indicating that women are harassed more severely online when compared to men (Duffy et al, 2022: Pew Research Center, 2021: Suzor et al., 2019), women respondents were less likely to experience psychological impacts from harassment when psychological impacts were examined alone as the dependent variable. Feminist theory was applied to social media platforms in this study, predicting that the gender inequality of the terrestrial world will follow users into the online world. It could be likely that the gendered harassment that women face offline has prepared them for the gendered harassment they face online. Therefore, because women may be used to being harassed online and offline, they may not experience psychological impacts such as depression or anxiety as often in response to online harassment. It could be likely that the harassment women face in the terrestrial world has a more immediate impact on their mental health as it perpetrated directly in their physical presence. The reaction to a comment physically in person may induce stronger mental health impacts, compared to the if the same comment was made online. And while they may not have immediate mental reactions, they could still be experiencing long term physical symptoms from the harassment they face online. The stress of harassment may induce physical symptoms over time even if the person is not reacting mentally.

As for all other models where gender was not significant, the explanation for why the predictions of feminist theory is not supported could be related to the harassment scale used to measure online harassment behaviors. Wilson et al. (2022) created a list of behaviors based on how 33 other studies measured online harassment. The wide collection of studies referenced varied in gendering of their samples. While some studies examined the harassment of women only, many studies analyzed the harassment of both genders. Therefore, it is possible that men and women commit harassment and experience harassment differently, causing some of the scale items to cancel each other out. More detail will be provided in the limitations section.

Influencers
The OLS regression model testing if social media influencers and female social influencers will experience greater economic impacts indicates that online harassment is associated with economic consequences for all influencers, though no significant gender difference was found. Social media platforms profit from the presence of influencers on their sites. Increased user engagement means increased profit for these corporations regardless if the engagement is causing harm to those who are economically vulnerable. This economic vulnerability mirrors that of terrestrial workers. Both influencers and terrestrial workers are dependent on their workplaces to support their livelihoods. Research on terrestrial workplace harassment found negative economic consequences to be associated. This study also found that influencers who experience harassment also experience economic impacts. The key difference is

that there is no federal legislation influencers can rely upon if they would like to fight for retribution and regain some of the economic capital that they lost.

Having an active sponsorship was significant in the OLS regression model testing if experiencing psychological and physiological effects will cause greater economic impacts. If a respondent has an active corporate sponsorship, their potential for economic gain and loss online becomes heightened. The very nature of product promotion increases the influencer's visibility to their audience as they are creating an increased amount of content for other users to comment on. This could potentially allow for increased risk of experiencing harassment and the impacts that follow. Because harassment is found to be a commonplace occurrence on social media (Adams, 2018) more content that is visible and engages the attention of users puts the creator at risk of experiencing more harassment. This may require more economic loss for influencers such as taking breaks from posting and loss of corporate sponsorships as noted by Hassan et al. (2018). Studies examining the impacts of online harassment for regular users have indicated that responses to online harassment include psychological symptoms like depression and anxiety or physical symptoms such as loss of sleep or headaches (Begotti & Maran, 2019). These phenomena require medical treatment such as medication or therapy, causing those impacted to spend money if they want their symptoms reduced (Villacampa & Pujols, 2018: Maple et al., 2011).

The negative mental health impacts of social media users, links to bullying behaviors and unregulated emotions (Craig et al, 2020: Mitropoulou, Karagianni & Thomadakis, 2022) will likely also continue to play a part in online harassment prevalence as it creates motivated offenders. Because social media use is becoming prevalent throughout the world (Kaur et al., 2021) and social media influencers must engage on social media to further their careers, there is

a growing base of victims that are instantly accessible. The physical interactions that Cohen &
Felson (1979) wrote about are no longer required for routine activities to cause victimization.

Location

It is important to highlight that location was found to have a significant negative
relationship with harassment in the OLS regression model testing that women would experience
greater levels of harassment than men. Respondents were less likely to experience harassment
behaviors in this model if they were located in North America. Because the model testing
hypothesis 1 was run on the entire sample, the majority of whom did not experience the
harassment behaviors listed on the Wilson et al., 2022 scale, also happen to be located in North
America. Therefore, in the total sample size, most had not experienced harassment while most
respondents were also from North America, causing location to appear as an insignificant
predictor of harassment. This changes as the sample is filtered to only respondents who had
experienced the harassment behaviors listed by Wilson et al. (2022).

Location also had a significant negative relationship in the model testing if greater levels
of online harassment will be associated with greater economic impacts. Respondents located in
North America were less likely to experience economic impacts. This may be because of access
to healthcare and greater economic opportunity in North America. The prevalence of health
insurance in the United States and Canada may allow psychiatric medication and therapy to be
relatively inexpensive or even free, allowing for a smaller amount of economic impact reported
by respondents from North America.

However, location was found to be a stronger predictor of the combined impacts of
online harassment. When the psychological, physiological and economic impacts of online
harassment are tested together empirically as one variable, the degree of potential impacts
increases for those who live in North America. This may be linked to the prevalence of internet

access and the emphasis on free speech in North America. Internet access is concentrated to many areas of the United States and Canada. Also, the United States and Canada have democratic government that protect free speech rights, emboldening users to speak freely online, even if their comments are negative towards others. Therefore, harassment levels may be higher in North America causing an increase in harassment impacts for users.

Other Findings

The OLS regression model testing that an increase in online harassment will be associated with an increase in economic impacts indicated that using the block feature made respondents less likely to experience economic impacts. However, the block feature was not significant in the other models, testing the relationship between harassment and psychological impacts and physiological impacts. It could be that though the block feature does not stop all harassment from being visible to a respondent, as noted by the high harassment mean in the sample descriptive table, it does block the comments that are likely most severe and disliked by the respondent. If a user takes the time to add certain words or phrases to a platform's word blocking tool, it is likely because these particular words or phrases are especially offensive to them. Therefore, users may be successful in blocking the types of harassment that induce strong reactions that could eventually lead to economic investment in coping mechanisms. Their need for therapy or psychiatric medications could decrease with the use of the blocking feature even though other forms of less severe harassment (to them) are still occurring. What remains is harassing comments that do not require respondents to invest in coping strategies though they are unpleasant to encounter.

Because the content volume is so vast on social media (Farid, 2018), platforms have placed the burden on users to protect themselves. This is why the block feature and reporting mechanisms exist. However, the block feature does not appear to be effective at protecting users from experiencing online harassment generally but it does appear to protect users from the economic impacts associated with experiencing harassment when economic impacts is tested alone as an independent variable. Other controls that attempted to address online exposure such as posting content with the respondent's face, reading comments made on posts had no impact across the other models. It was thought that all of these behaviors require a certain level of respondent engagement with other users, forcing them to observe the harassing behaviors of others. This may have to do with a flaw in the design of the study, which will be discussed further in the limitations section.

Limitations

The sampling for this research was not random therefore, the results are not generalizable. Because the influencer population was selected from the author's Instagram account, there is a sampling bias that overrepresents health/fitness and fashion/beauty content.

Harassment and combined impacts were self-reported by respondents. Using a Likert scale in survey research allows participants to be subjective in their responses, making it difficult to measure behaviors and impacts in a precise manner. The term "often" could mean once per day to one person while meaning three times today to another. Therefore, there is no exact measurement for any of the impacts or experiences presented in this study. Though there are scores associated with the results of the scales, the results do not show precise frequencies.

This study did not ask if respondents had public or private profiles. Closing a profile off to only approved users would likely impact the levels of harassment that a person experiences. Because an influencer's earning potential increases with the number of followers, it is likely that all influencers will have public profiles where users can follow easily. Those aspiring to be influencers will likely follow suit. However, because this study included average users (non-influencers), they do not have the same incentives to keep a public profile. Failing to control for this may have caused certain variables in the model to read as insignificant in a private profile that would be significant in a public profile. If a respondent is sharing face content often to a group of followers that they have approved, it could be less likely that their approved audience would say something disparaging. Therefore, using the block feature in this situation would likely not have an impact on how a person with a private account experiences harassment.

The social media behaviors of the respondent were not tested in this study, only their experiences. Respondent behaviors may contribute to harassment exposure risk. For instance, respondents who post more often (like in the case of having an active sponsorship) may have an increased risk of being harassed. Respondents who harass others online more often may also receive increased harassment in return. The nature of posts (subject, tone, language) is also important to consider. Inflammatory posts that are controversial may cause the respondent to receive more harassment from their audience. The controls of this study only examined what respondents experience from others and not how they are interacting with others, which could be more important for understanding what makes respondents experience harassment behaviors.

The Wilson et al. (2022) online harassment scale used in this study was generated from a collection of other studies that analyzed the harassment victimization of both genders. The scale did not consider the different ways that men and women may be harassed. For example, men may receive more physical threats (Pew Research Center, 2021) due to the socialized acceptability of men being more violent (Becker et al., 2020), while women are not reporting death threats but sexual harassment instead. Santos et al. (2021) found that women are more likely to participate in cyberstalking behaviors as an attempt to build or maintain an intimate relationship with the victim. Therefore, it is possible that men and women commit and experience harassment differently, causing some of the scale items to cancel each other out and gender to appear insignificant.

The content type variable could have been dichotomized in a way that more accurately represented the experiences of genders. For example, the items in the one category included health/fitness, fashion/beauty as they were the largest categories. Parenting and family could have also been added to this group as it is largely a feminine trope. However, it is far less likely that criticism about parenting ideas or family activities would affect someone in the same way as a personal attack on their appearance or fitness level. For example, someone offering fitness tips might be subject to body shaming which is more hurtful to most women than an attack on their parenting technique. Still, the nuance of gendered content may have been lost with this decision.

Finally, economic impacts for users and influencers were measured on one economic impact scale. The economic vulnerability is greater for influencers, making their economic impacts different from that of a regular user. Though there may be some overlap in experiences, influencers and aspiring influencers can potentially experience long-term career impacts, which can be framed as economic impacts, that would not apply to a regular social media user. For example, taking a break from posting in response to harassment behaviors is on the economic impacts scale used in this study. However, this choice would not yield economic consequences for a regular user but may equate to a loss of views and engagements for an influencer, resulting in the loss of income. When regular users responded with "always, often, sometimes or rarely" to taking a break from posting, this study was labeling these responses as an economic impact, even when this may not have entirely been the case.

Policy implications

This research shows that online harassment negatively impacts users who experience it. The United States needs to amend the "good faith" concept within section 230 of the Communications Decency Act. The United States must begin setting measurable, future content moderation goals for corporations to strive for. For example, corporations should be required to remove sexual content that was shared without the user's consent within a specific timeframe after the report was made. That would be acting in good faith.

Content moderation requirements should follow the realistic development pace of monitoring technologies (such as artificial intelligence and machine learning) and allow time for the hiring of additional human monitors. The intention of Section 230 of the CDA back in 1996 was to ensure that the internet could grow, unimpeded by governmental oversight. Needless to say, this has been achieved. In present times, the United States government needs to begin to find ways to hold social media platforms accountable, such as Meta and Instagram, for known negative impacts on users.

In the case of influencers, their workplace is social media. Though they are not employees of the platforms where they work, they acquire revenue for these platforms. Therefore, social media corporations benefit financially from influencer participation and should incur some responsibility for how harassment negatively impacts this population. Terrestrial workplace harassment mirrors some of the observations found in this study like negative economic impact and negative emotional impact. Under existing workplace legislation, social media corporations are not liable for the harassment that influencers face. Also, applying United States workplace legislation is very limiting as influencing is a global profession and not all influencers are United States citizens. Instead of attempting to apply the same protections to social media influencers that are provided by the 1964 Civil Rights Act to terrestrial workers, new legislation should be written that requires social media corporations to provide a benefits package to influencers. This package should be similar to the ones offered to terrestrial workers. Benefits such as healthcare, paid vacation days and mental health resources should be provided by platforms to influencers who meet certain criteria. Such criteria could include a minimum level of advertising revenue generated for the corporation, a minimum number of subscribers or certain number of advertising contracts signed within one year. A portion of the budget, like the $1 Billion that Meta (Facebook) invested into influencers back in 2022 (Bradley, 2022), could be used to help pay for benefits that work to help influencers mitigate the negative impacts of online harassment. Afterall, an influencer that is creating will continue to make the corporation money. Offering support to influencers when needed is a good first step in offsetting some of the negative economic impacts that come with experiencing harassment.

Suggestions for future research

Because gender was shown to be insignificant in this study but shown to be significant in other studies, more research is needed to understand the differences in how men, women are harassed online. In addition to understanding how people experience harassment, more research needs to be done on how people perpetuate harassment. According to PEW research center, being physically threatened online impacts men more often than women (Pew Research Center, 2021). A volatile man online may send death threats to a man and sexually harassing messages to a woman, so the type of harassment might differ for men and women which might explain the mixed findings.

Future research should inquire about the respondent's harassment behavior in addition to how they are harassed. This could provide more insight into how genders harass each other.

Following the logic of feminist theory, asking men specific questions about how they view certain types of female influencers could provide more clarity around if harassment is coming from a place of male privilege or sexist ideologies. Further, asking respondents about the gender of the users harassing them to see how gender changes the type of harassment perpetuated would be a good next step in developing the significance of gender within this scholarship.

One factor that was not explored in this study was the respondent's relationship or living status. Being harassed by a stranger online may be more stressful for someone who is in a committed relationship as they do not want to be involved with a person who shows disrespect to their romantic commitments. If a person is not in a committed relationship, they may find repeated "romantic" messages from a stranger to be intriguing or even annoying instead of feeling harassed and unsafe. On the contrary, for a person who lives alone, repeated harassment messages may induce increased levels of fear for their safety. Becker et al., (2020) found that women, who experience online cyberstalking behaviors more often, are also more likely to perceive repeated messages from an unknown man as dangerous behavior. But they also found that this is not always true of men who receive repeated messages from unknown women. This study, like the current study, also did not account for relationship status which is likely to impact how a person feels in response to repeated harassment messages when in a committed relationship and if this effect is the same across genders.

More research is needed to understand if using the block feature has financial consequences for influencers such as decreasing their engagement metrics. Companies use a variety of metrics to select which influencers they would like to work with and engagement percentages is one of them (Bradley, 2022). An influencer with an engaged audience likely means more revenue potential for the investing company. However, social media algorithms are largely secretive and seem to favor negative and volatile content (Walter, 2022). Blocking negative engagements could very well result in a loss of content circulation and income for influencers and the companies that partner with them. There may not be a clear way to study the impacts of the block feature without the help of the platforms in question. If protecting oneself from harassment by using the block feature, especially from the negative impacts that cost the recipient money to deal with (as this study shows) also cause the recipient to lose income, social media platforms have an ethical obligation to change. Harm and protection from harm, especially at one's place of work, should not cost individuals money.

TikTok is another popular social media platform for regular users and influencers alike. Many influencers tend to work on a multitude of platforms in order to maximize their income potential. For example, popular nutrition influencer Abbey Sharp shares content on YouTube, Instagram and TikTok. Users can follow her on all three platforms if they desire and view differently curated content on each different app. Because TikTok is a Chinese platform, future research should study the combined impacts of online harassment for users and influencers on TikTok specifically and compare it with their experiences on American platforms. The differences in Chinese internet legislation, software development techniques, and culture may create a different social media experience compared to American platforms like Instagram. This research should also consider the working environments of influencers and if they receive different treatment on Tik-Tok, or any other future emerging platform that is outside of the United States.

All sources of potential influencer income were not included in this study. Around eighty percent of harassed influencers had an active sponsorship. Other sources of income options such as affiliate links or personal brand products promotion were not asked about. It could be that having a more passive source of income, like affiliate links, where the influencer gets paid if a follower clicks on it, does not require as much audience engagement therefore decreasing the amount of harassment that they experience overall. There could be methods of generating income that make an influencer more vulnerable to negative economic impact. Future studies should compare active sponsorships, promotion of personal brand products, affiliate links and other ways of generating income to see which of these invites harassment behaviors and increases the likelihood of experiencing negative impacts.

Considering that most of the controls addressing internet behavior in this study (posting face content, time spent online, content type, reading comments) were not significant in any OLS regression model that was run, more research is needed to understand which online participation behaviors make users vulnerable to harassment. Questions about the intention of or language around user posts, how often they post and if they comment often on the post of others were not included in this study. Essentially, the focus was on what the respondents experienced on social media and not how they were behaving on social media. It could be that the frequency at which a user posts or comments, along with the subject matter of the post and comments influences the level of harassment that they experience. Future research should study user behavior, along with user experience to determine if certain behaviors increase vulnerability to harassment and its impacts. Ideally, a standardized social media user behavior scale would be developed and tested across many different studies.

The economic impacts scale for this study was generated by impacts observed by other authors, including Maple et al. (2011) who found that in the United Kingdom, the financial consequences of online harassment reported by respondents were "lost money, legal expenses, therapy expenses, and using paid leave" and Hassan et al. (2018) who that found from interviewing a small number of influencers that "account closure, loss of brand deal" are economic impacts that specifically impact influencers. Currently, there is no standardized economic impact scale used when measuring impacts from online harassment. This study supports that online harassment has the potential to yield negative financial consequences so future research should work to develop standardized economic impact scales for users and a scale specifically for influencers that also addresses the consequences of potential career impacts.

Future research should examine the impacts of online harassment in a longitudinal study. Other researchers should conduct longitudinal studies to see if there are long term consequences to experiencing harassment and its impacts. Also, longitudinal studies on harassment and its impact on the career trajectories of influencers should be conducted as well.

This study was a cross-sectional study and did not control for causal order. Therefore, it cannot be concluded if the harassment or the impacts came first. For example, having anxiety or depression may cause a user to behave in a certain way online that invites harassment from other users. Therefore, to truly assess that harassment causes impacts, other researchers should conduct longitudinal studies that control for the causal order of anxiety, depression and other health problems in question at the beginning of the study. It should be examined if these elements change over time in response to experiencing harassment behaviors.

Finally, future research should study how both race/ethnicity and location influence the level of harassment that someone experiences. This study did not examine race, only the location of respondents. It was originally thought that location would impact the gendered experiences of respondents per the World Bank ranking of countries by gender equality. For example, women in Africa or Asia may experience elevated levels of harassment online due a culture of gender inequality in some regions. Because location was a significant factor associated with economic impacts in this research, additional research is needed to understand if harassment is linked to internet access/use or if it is linked to the values of the population that lives there. Though race/ethnicity is diverse in North America, adding race into that analysis would likely provide more clarity as to who gets harassed, not just where people get harassed. It could be that race is linked to location when it comes to increased levels of online harassment.

Conclusion

This study adds to the literature by highlighting that online harassment does have combined negative psychological, physiological and economic impacts. When impacts are examined in concert, the influence of harassment is stronger. Also, location becomes a stronger predictor of harassment impacts as well. This is cause for concern as people continue to utilize social media platforms not only to stay connected but also to establish careers and gain income. Social media is free to access and removes the traditional barriers to economic success such as education, industry specific tenure, and the need to live near an employment location. Other research has shown that excessive social media use has negative health outcomes, women experience online abuse more often and the algorithms on social media applications, which are meant to be addictive, tend to favor the circulation of negative and inflammatory content. All these things are harmful, and this study adds to the list of harms done by social media by highlighting that online harassment is associated with negative combined impacts, including psychological and physiological impacts, which in turn cost money to remedy. Under current legislation, United States based social media corporations have no legal obligation to explore these harms further and attempt to reduce them. They also have no obligation according to international legislation, which means that these harms can proliferate throughout the world.

Having an active sponsorship makes someone more likely to have negative economic impacts that requires further research. Active corporate sponsorships are one way that influencers gain income on social media platforms. If making income on social media allows a person to be more vulnerable to negative economic impacts, especially when harassed, more research is required to understand why this problem exists and if it can be remedied. Influencers are not protected by anti-harassment laws like all other traditional workers employed in the United States. Therefore, the question of who should protect the rights of influencers is raised. Should it be the United States government, the platforms themselves, or a combination of both? Current legislation both domestically and internationally does not adequately answer these questions. This is problematic as online harassment has known psychological, physiological and economic harms which need to be addressed at some level.

At present, more research is needed to understand the nuances of how genders perpetuate harassment and experience harassment in order to measure true prevalence of gendered harassment. The scales used in this study could have offered behaviors that are experienced almost exclusively by men and conversely other behaviors that are mostly experienced by women, causing the scores to essentially cancel each other out. More research is also required to further understand why women may be less likely to experience psychological impacts but do not present as resilient to the physiological, economic or combined impacts from harassment.

Location proved to be a stronger predictor of harassment when the combined effects were tested empirically as one variable. Being located in North America indicates that a respondent is more likely to experience psychological, physiological and combined impacts. Additional research is required to understand why being located in North America does not make a respondent more likely to experience economic impacts. Location and gender will likely need to be examined together as different locations offer different gender norms and may influence what determines culturally acceptable behavior online.

Overall, social media is both harmful and beneficial for humanity. This study highlights that experiencing harassment behaviors online is associated with negative psychological, physiological and economic impacts. Harassment and location become stronger predictors when impacts are examined in concert. Social media platforms have a social responsibility to address the harms that they are both creating and perpetuating. Legislation has not caught up to this fact. The world is becoming increasingly more dependent on the internet, and social media use is included as well. As internet access expands internationally, so will the benefits and the harms of social media. If social platforms want to continue to be a profitable workplace for influencers, they should attempt to reduce or remedy the negative impacts on this population. Online harassment is harmful and should no longer be tolerated, especially because it can be framed as a form of workplace discrimination for influencers. According to the United States Civil Rights Act of 1964, it is a human right to be able to work free of harassment. This should be true of the online world as well.

www.ingramcontent.com/pod-product-compliance
Lightning Source LLC
LaVergne TN
LVHW020927200726
843506LV00011B/1850